Smack-Dab in the Midlife Zone

Inspiration for Women in the Middle

Praise for Smack-Dab in the Midlife Zone

Many of us who are bogged down in the busy motherhood years sometimes look into the future and imagine life after mountains of laundry and running Mom's Taxi Service—or we gaze ahead wistfully to our retirement years. But unexpected emotions often arise as those moments approach, sometimes accompanied with a fearful "Now what?"

In *Smack-Dab in the Midlife Zone*, Leigh Ann Thomas walks us through this stage of life with encouragement, laughter, and godly principles. A must-read!

—**Michelle Cox**, author and contributor to over twenty books, including *Just 18 Summers* and the *When God Calls the Heart* devotional series

With depth of heart and full of every emotion, Leigh Ann Thomas creatively captures the realities every woman "in the middle" experiences. Don't be fooled by the moments of laughter—they will be followed by notes of introspection that will move you to the Cross.

Smack-Dab in the Midlife Zone is the perfect blend of story and inspiration that connects me to women I have yet to meet. Even better, the Holy Spirit flows out of the words on the page to convict me and love me.

Whether your journey is just beginning, or you are smack in the middle of the middle—Leigh Ann will befriend and help you on your way as she points you to the One who knows and loves you best!

—**Shelley Pierce**, pastor's wife, ministry leader, author of multiple books, including *Sweet Moments for the Pastor's Wife*

Leigh Ann Thomas is the real thing—an authentic Christian in a world full of pretenders. Using her gifts to write, present thought-provoking

dramas, and lead conferences, Leigh Ann touches everyone with whom she comes in contact with words that challenge them to do significant self-reflection using God's word as their measuring instrument. The same is true in the pages of this book. Her words will make you smile and maybe tear up a bit as you recognize yourself in them, but mostly, they will push you to truly seek God's best in your current season of life.
—**Caroline McManus Jones**, retired missionary to Chile, inspirational speaker, and women's ministry leader

What you see is what you get—literally—with Leigh Ann Thomas's latest book, *Smack-Dab in the Midlife Zone!* Leigh Ann's honesty, humility, and humor will speak straight to your heart as you join her on this inevitable journey into the ever-changing process of aging. As you read, you will be encouraged to find that you are not alone on this daily-roller-coaster road trip. And you will definitely be inspired by glimpses into Leigh Ann's real-life escapades, her heart-felt prayers, and her challenges for quiet reflections while on your own faith journey.
—**Phyllis Elliott Elvington**, Bible teacher, speaker, and multi-published author

Leigh Ann's words stir me deeply as I also experience midlife. Her skillful writing mixes wisdom and humor, allowing the reader to process this sudden season with a biblical perspective and tender amusement. Leigh Ann's devotion to the Lord plus her ability to lead others toward Him make this book a powerful resource for middle-aged women.
—**Emily Wickham**, author, speaker, mentor, and founder of *Proclaiming Him to Women Ministries*

In *Smack-Dab in the Midlife Zone*, Leigh Ann Thomas takes the traditional mindset of being "middle aged" and turns it on its head. She uses a wonderful combination of humor and personal stories, all centered around the Word of God, to help us navigate this phase of life that is filled with so much change—by depending on and glorifying our Lord who never changes. You will receive encouragement and purpose for every situation, from dealing with the emotion of children leaving the nest, to the weariness of caring for aging parents, as each page

intentionally leads you to refreshing Scriptures and strengthening prayer.
—**Rev. Matt Martin**, pastor, Cool Springs Baptist Church, Sanford, NC

Using both wisdom and wit, Leigh Ann Thomas offers readers an insightful glimpse into the mystery of midlife. The melding of real-life stories with scripture extends hope and encouragement to women of all ages.
—**Cathy Baker**, author of the *Pauses for the Vacationing Soul* devotional series

Smack-Dab in the Midlife Zone

Inspiration for Women in the Middle

Leigh Ann Thomas

PUBLISHING THE POSITIVE

ELK LAKE PUBLISHING INC
Plymouth, Massachusetts

Cover and Interior Design: Derinda Babcock

Editor(s): Sue Fairchild, Deb Haggerty

Author Represented by Credo Communications LLC

PUBLISHED BY: Elk Lake Publishing, Inc., 35 Dogwood Dr., Plymouth, MA 02360, 2019

_____

Library Cataloging Data

Names: Thomas, Leigh Ann (Leigh Ann Thomas)

Smack-Dab in the Midlife Zone: Inspiration for Women in the Middle / Leigh Ann Thomas

144 p. 23cm × 15cm (9in × 6 in.)

Description: Women in the middle often feel lost—their kids are grown, but they're too young to retire. *Smack-Dab in the Midlife Zone* offers encouragement to women in that stage of life.

Identifiers: ISBN-13: 978-1-950051-71-7 (trade) | 978-1-950051-72-4 (POD) | 978-1-950051-73-1 (e-book.)

Key Words: Middle age, Empty Nest, Self-Esteem, Life Changes, Future Plans, Relationships, Religion

LCCN: 2019940506 Nonfiction

Dedication

In memory of my grandmother,
Almeda Thomas Nall,
whose joy and laughter have surely
enriched the halls of heaven.

She selects wool and flax

and works with eager hands.

She makes linen garments and sells them,

and supplies the merchants with sashes.

She is clothed with strength and dignity;

she can laugh at the days to come.

(Proverbs 31:13, 24–25)

Table of Contents

Acknowledgments

The creation of a book can be a curious journey packed with extreme delight and a touch of *what-in-the-world-am-I-doing?* Thankfully, the Lord provides traveling companions to increase the joy and to temper the angst. Over the past months, my life has been enriched by those who have used their gifts and abilities to encourage this grateful writer and to fine-tune this manuscript.

My deepest gratitude to:

The Elk Lake Publishing Inc. family, including Editor-in-Chief Deb Haggerty, editor Sue Fairchild, and graphic designer Derinda Babcock, for your Christ-centered values and professionalism. Thank you for your enthusiasm for this work. May God continue to use you to further his purposes. Also, Tim Beals and Credo Communications for your willingness to stand behind *Smack-Dab* and to speak for me.

My sisters in the faith who shared their hearts and their stories for this manuscript—midlife never looked so beautiful! You live with vision and passion and I pray God uses your journeys to touch others in his name.

InTheQuiver.com cohorts, Hilary Hall and Marcy Martin, and fellow wordsmiths, Shelley Pierce and Charla Matthews—you keep me accountable and push me to stretch and grow in my writing, and in my Christ-walk. You are precious friends and I praise God for you.

My first-draft reader and life-long cheerleader—my mom, Atha Nall. Your creative energy and giving heart continue to teach and to inspire me. You are loved.

My beloved daughters and treasured friends—Laura, Mary, and Katie. What a joy to share our creative adventures! I'll be cheering (seriously, jumping up and down) as you continue to explore God's plans and as you lay your talents at the feet of Jesus. You have my forever mom-love and my constant prayers.

God's most incredible gift and blessing—my sweetheart—Roy. I can't imagine midlife, or *any* season, without you by my side. Thank you for wanting God's best for us and for insisting that I truly *live*. I love you and I praise God for our priceless years (minutes?) of marriage. You're rather awesome, my love.

The Author of all love and creativity—my Savior, Redeemer, Counselor, and Friend. You are my purpose and my life. Abba, Father, I lift my hands in praise. All glory is yours.

See, I am doing a new thing! Now it springs up;
do you not perceive it?
I am making a way in the wilderness
and streams in the wasteland.

(Isaiah 43:19)

A "Hair" Brained Search

Being confident of this, that he who began a good work in
you will carry it on to completion until the day of Christ
Jesus. (Phil. 1:6)

The relationship began online.

I saw his picture—soulful brown eyes, longing expression—and my
heart responded in a tsunami of emotion. We had to meet.

Three days and a hundred and fifty miles later, I perched on a tiny
bench and waited for the furry answer to my prayers. My heart skipped
in anticipation as my gaze traveled from the pint-sized water dish in the
corner to the myriad toys scattered across the floor. My knee bounced with
nervous energy while I brushed rogue doggy-hairs from the bench and
fought an oncoming sneeze.

As the minutes ticked by, a shaft of doubt broke through my eagerness.
Lord, what am I doing here?

A woman entered the room, and my attention snapped to the ball of
fur in her arms. I reached to receive her bundle-of-love while my gathering
sneeze reached critical mass.

My allergic outburst rocked the room.

Two hours of indecision later, I wearily climbed in the car for the
three-hour trip home—sans Mr. Soulful Brown Eyes. Incredibly, I repeated
the trip a few weeks later. But this time, I claimed the ball of fur for my
own.

Twenty-four hours after that, I gave the little fellow to someone who
provided a sweet life of silk pillows and a warm lap—and who could love
him without breaking out in a red itchy rash.

I didn't want a dog.

I didn't *need* a dog.

The pointless trips and weeks of irrational indecision were symptoms of a deeper problem—a search—an endless seeking of something to fill a vague sense of emptiness. An emptiness that had grown to absurd proportions and maintained a stranglehold on my life.

My world had been in transition for several years. Our three daughters were growing at warp speed—moving into the high school and college years. One daughter's wedding was months away.

The familiar role of needed-all-the-time mom was slipping away, and the ground seemed to shift beneath my feet. I felt restless. Anxious. A mom without a mission. Life was changing, and I didn't care for it. At all. My thoughts were stuck in a continuous loop: Who am I? What is my purpose in this life-season? Where do I fit in?

I detested the words "middle age," but the resigned smirk of the woman in the mirror couldn't be denied. Where was the girl with dreams, plans, and goals? Where was her joy of walking with the Lord in complete abandon?

In my I-can-fix-this mentality, a new purpose was born. I would fill the emptiness with activity. I said "yes" to whatever was asked—from extra church activities, to mission trips, to a part-time job. All good things. But each morning upon waking, I reached beside the bed and pulled on the weight of "something's not right."

What did it look like to be at odds with God's will during this season? Tears. Excuses. An unsettled spirit.

Like a toddler who has lost sight of her daddy, my heart cried, "Lord, where are you? What now?"

Soon after the puppy fiasco, in emotional exhaustion, I fell at the feet of Jesus and unleashed the pent-up sobs of a broken and restless heart. With his strength, I surrendered my feeble attempts to refill the growing void. As the Holy Spirit whispered assurances to the deepest places of my heart, I realized my Lord would be the only one able and worthy to fill and sustain me during this new life season.

Yes, life was changing—but through the power of his Word, God reminded me his plans and purposes didn't end when my children began their own journeys or when my pear shape developed a pear shape.

This life-season wasn't the end, but a beautiful, magnificent beginning. The God of "all things new" wanted to do a "new thing" in me. The time

was now to rediscover my role in God's kingdom. To seek his heart and to leap into the next steps of this faith-adventure.

Perhaps you woke one morning and realized a huge chunk of time slipped by overnight. Every packed-with-activity day has been the same for so long you were lulled into thinking life would always be this way. Your son has moved out on his own, or your daughter has started college in another city. A wedding is on the horizon. Your parents are experiencing health problems and need you more and more.

You meet the gaze of the woman in the mirror and notice a touch of restlessness. What's-always-been slipped away when you weren't paying attention and left you feeling dazed and slightly panicked.

But in spite of what your senses tell you, this is not the end of a life of vibrancy, purpose, and joy. Your story is part of God's greater story, and the best is still to come.

The God who promises to finish what he started is ready with outstretched arms. He knows this packed-with-transition season can be infused with growth, discovery, and edge-of-your-seat adventure. The only requirements? A child-like trust and a heart of wonder and anticipation.

Our Lord is waiting. Grab his hand and hold on tight.

We have exploring to do!

Lord, I admit to feeling a little lost right now. My life is changing so fast, and I want to hold on to what I've always known. But Lord, I know you created me for joyful, purposeful living. You never intended for me to live in the past, weighted with fear and uncertainty. You call me to deeper waters—to live in such a way that others are drawn to you. I'm unsure of the next steps, Father, but I trust in your love and I pray for your perfect peace.

In the Zone

Spend a few moments in quiet reflection before the Lord. What is your biggest struggle in this season? Where do your uncertainties lie? Talk to Jesus as if he's sitting right next to you (see Psalm 34:18, Psalm 16:8). Share your heart and ask for strength to take the next steps in your faith journey.

Soaring in the Dry Places

I will make rivers flow on barren heights, and springs within the valleys. I will turn the desert into pools of water, and the parched ground into springs. (Isaiah 41:18)

Every step forward took us a half step back. Before us stretched an endless sea of sand, myriad dunes rising and falling against the blue of an early autumn sky. The sun hung bold and fierce and added to the illusion of desert solitude.

As my husband and I explored the otherworldly hills of Jockey's Ridge, NC, we could easily imagine we were miles from civilization. Strong winds whipped around us, and I squinted to keep tiny granules of sand from stinging my eyes.

I made a three hundred sixty degree turn and searched for signs of the bustling seaside village of Nags Head I knew to be beyond the dunes. From opposite sides, the Atlantic Ocean and the Roanoke Sound beckoned with promises of cool waters and endless recreational opportunities, but here we felt dwarfed by the mounds of nothingness. A complete lack of water, vegetation, or man-made structures.

What a barren place.

Oh, haven't we been there! A place where our souls feel dry and parched. A place where every step forward is followed by a backward slide, leaving us feeling weary and frustrated.

Our hearts search for signs of life and growth—a bit of green in a world of brown and gray. Our eyes grow weary as our gazes scan the horizon—looking, longing for a simple touch of color.

We wonder, is there purpose here? Can we possibly grow in this wasteland?

The psalmist's heart beat with the same questions as he placed his impoverished spirit before the living God. "As the deer pants for streams of water, so my soul pants for you, my God. My soul thirsts for God, for the living God. When can I go and meet with God?" (Psalm 42:1–2). The next verses provide insight into his tattered world. He writes of his tears day and night, and of the ridicule of mockers. He remembers times of joyful worship when he would lead others in shouts of thanksgiving on the way to the house of God. He thinks of a rich, meaningful life, but in his present reality, those times seem lost forever.

And then verse five—words that shake me with their power.

This writer in despair poses a profound question and makes a gutsy decision.

"Why, my soul, are you downcast? Why so disturbed within me? Put your hope in God, for I will yet praise him, my Savior and my God" (Psalm 42:5).

Oh, how the first half of this verse reverberates through us! Why am I feeling this way? What is wrong with me? Will I ever feel "me" again?

We pause, startled by the psalmist's next words. *Put your hope in God.*

But, wait. We don't have all the answers. We don't know what lies ahead. *Put your hope in God, for I will yet praise him.*

Can we trust before we know?

Is there genuine hope in this dry place?

There's a fascinating component to the dunes of Jockey's Ridge. The outer layers are covered by sunbaked, shifting sands. But just underneath the surface, tiny granules of sand retain moisture through the seasons. That unseen amount of water prevents the dunes from being dislocated by the relentless battering of high winds.[1] In our Creator's perfect design, an anchor is provided.

Hope lives in the deep places.

The day of our hike, my husband and I topped a dune and our eyes widened at the bursts of color dotting the landscape. At the peak of an adjacent dune, a group gathered. Cheers and applause floated across the sea of sand as a woman, harnessed to a huge red and yellow kite, "flew" to the base of the dune.

We stared, mesmerized, as others were strapped to brilliant, colorful wings and in turn, surfed the air currents amidst screams of delight. They had discovered a joy-filled purpose for a dry, useless place.

They found a way to soar in the desert.

In spite of what we feel, may we remember that at the foundation of our present circumstances, there is a never-ending source of deep and abiding hope.

Oh, Father, how I long to trust you. To praise you in times of darkness, when I don't know every answer or when the future is confusing and unclear. This moment, I ask for strength to reach for you in the unknown. I love you, Father, and I choose to lift your name in worship. I want to soar in your faithfulness!

In the Zone

Read Psalm 42:1–5. In what ways do you identify with the psalmist? Following his example, list specific praises and thanksgivings to God. Ask God for courage to praise him in the unknown. In the coming days, make note of ways your praises strengthen your hope in Christ.

Who is That?

You are altogether beautiful, my darling; there is no flaw in you. (Song of Solomon 4:7)

When reading inspirational fiction, have you noticed that novelists use various techniques to let their readers "see" the appearance of a particular character? One of the more common methods is when the heroine gazes in a mirror, and the writer describes the scene.

The narrative might go something like this: *Eloise stood before the ornate antique mirror and attempted to corral her unruly mass of auburn curls. Large emerald eyes framed by impossibly long lashes stared back at her, and her gaze lowered demurely before returning to complete the self-appraisal. A small, straight nose with just the hint of freckles, smooth peaches and cream complexion, and full naturally-red lips completed her perusal.*

Eloise smiled at her reflection. "What a marvelous day to be young."

(Um, see why I'm not a novelist?)

There's not an abundance of middle-aged heroines in modern storytelling, but perhaps there should be. Can you imagine?

Leigh Ann stood before the fogged bathroom mirror and rubbed an eye-level circle with the side of her hand. She attempted to corral her flyaway blond/gray tresses as faded blue eyes, one lid slightly drooping, stared back at her. An average nose with hints of sun-damage, an uneven skin tone, and brand-new tiny lines at the corners of her mouth completed her perusal.

Leigh Ann sighed and crossed her eyes at the foggy reflection. "What a marvelous day to apply more makeup."

We know what God's Word says about real beauty—that God is more interested in our inner selves—the unfading beauty of a gentle and quiet spirit. But the physical changes in this life season are still tough to accept. Especially when we live in a youth-worshipping culture.

Value is placed on the young, the fit, and the attractive—and if we don't happen to fall into these categories, there's a quick solution available. Options abound: Hair color for those gray strands, creams and gels for the lines and puffiness, and endless weight loss options from diet and exercise gurus.

Society shouts—you may not be young and beautiful, but you can be. We'll help you turn back the clock! And the more we search for youth, the more unsettled and discontented we become. The image in the mirror can't compete with the barrage of images from magazine covers and social media.

What's a girl to do?

As women in our forties, fifties, sixties, and beyond, it's unrealistic to think we can compete physically with women half our age. But what if our mindsets shift from one of competition to one of joyful acceptance? What if we embrace this season, and with God's strength, commit to be our best?

Wouldn't we rather be a strong, confident woman—at any age—instead of a middle-aged woman trying to fit into a twenty-something life? Are there bits of treasure to be discovered in this season that were simply unavailable in our youth? Future chapters will continue this exploration.

If we are a part of God's bigger story, what does that mean for the here and now? Can we possibly counteract the pressures of living in a youth-obsessed culture with an eternal perspective?

Psalm 139:13–16 reads, "For you created my inmost being; you knit me together in my mother's womb. I praise you because I am fearfully and wonderfully made; your works are wonderful, I know that full well. My frame was not hidden from you when I was made in the secret place, when I was woven together in the depths of the earth. Your eyes saw my unformed body; all the days ordained for me were written in your book before one of them came to be."

Oh, how we are treasured by our Creator! From the moment we were woven together, God has loved us with an everlasting faithfulness. This incredible life journey, with all of its joys and hardships and changes, is designed to mold and shape us into the image of Christ.

With our finite vision, we see loss of physical beauty through natural aging.

With eternal and infinite vision, God looks at us and sees the splendor of his Son.

Every circumstance—both joys and hardships—has the potential to create in us unfading beauty and to propel us forward on our unique, God-ordained walks of faith.

Is there anything lovelier than a woman contented in Christ? A woman with spiritual fire—one who loves, serves, and reaches others for her Lord. "And walk in the way of love, just as Christ loved us and gave himself up for us as a fragrant offering and sacrifice to God" (Ephesians 5:2).

Let's continue to mine this unique time—looking past outward physical changes—to embrace a new place of depth and beauty. Because regardless of age, the closer we grow to our Lord, the more radiant we become.

Besides, the world needs a few good heroines.

Father, I don't want to become trapped in vanity and shallow living. Give me eyes to see beyond the surface effects of aging in this fallen world and to focus on the work you continue to complete in me. Oh, how I want to be more like you! I pray for courage to view every circumstance through your heart and for wisdom to keep an eternal perspective each day.

In the Zone

In what ways have you bought into the world's view of youth and beauty? Meditate on the following verses: Ephesians 2:10, Matthew 10:29–31, and 2 Corinthians 5:17. How does God's view of you alter your vision of true value and loveliness?

What Lies Beneath

Create in me a pure heart, O God, and renew a steadfast spirit within me. (Psalm 51:10)

A snowstorm in central North Carolina is a rare and fascinating event. Businesses and schools close at the first snowflake, twenty-four-hour news coverage rules the local television stations, and regular life slows to a crawl.

Moms rummage through drawers looking for gloves to cover each tiny hand and dads wonder where they stashed the snow shovel they bought a decade ago. Snow angels and snow men become works of art. Enough snow cream is prepared to enjoy some now and to freeze a pint or two for later.

In contrast to our northern neighbors, snowfall events in the south are not a drudgery but a cause for delight and celebration. Nature whispers, "Be still and worship the Creator of all this."

As the frozen glory continues to fall, the brown and gray, barren and brittle world is clothed in glimmering white. The ugliness of rot and decay is transformed into breathtaking beauty.

We gaze at the loveliness and marvel at the transformation. And for a moment, we forget what's beneath the blanket of white. For a moment, we embrace the vision of purity and perfection.

But we know what's coming. The storehouse of winter wonder closes its doors as temperatures rise and the sun spreads its warmth. The mirage of purity fades and we discover that this old world wasn't transformed at all—only covered for a time.

The decay remains.

The winter dressing is an engaging picture of God's redemptive work on our behalf. His blood-red sacrifice covered our dirty, brittle hearts of sin and decay. But unlike nature's temporary mantle, God's covering is eternal and will never flee from the heat—from the stress and hardships of this life. "For he has rescued us from the dominion of darkness and brought us into the kingdom of the Son he loves, in whom we have redemption, the forgiveness of sins" (Colossians 1:13–14).

Part of the jolt of this season of life is that we've been distracted by the blur and busyness of our every day. Our Christ-focus has wavered, and we've allowed doubt to seep into the corners of our frazzled minds. The magnificence of God's redemptive work, the thought of which used to take our breath away, has become lost in our struggle to find our footing.

With fragile joy and tentative steps, we approach our rescuer. Lord, are you sure the stains are gone? I remember what used to be there—the grit and grime and ugliness. Will your covering be—enough? What if the blackened areas show through?

The One who formed the earth and knit us together in our mother's womb and surrendered to the pain of metal spikes—this same One—pulls us close and whispers to our spirit.

"Child, the stains are not simply covered. They are no more. I have removed them and no longer count them against you. When I look at you, I see the righteousness of my Son—beautiful and beloved" (based on 2 Corinthians 5:21).

Doubting the validity of our foundation hinders us from taking the next steps in our faith adventure. The time is now to ponder, believe, and accept God's glorious, unimaginable, and life-giving act of redemption on our behalf.

What lies beneath the covering of white? The irreplaceable treasures of a clean heart and a steadfast spirit—precious in his sight.

Oh Father, may I never forget what it cost you to take this dirty, lifeless heart of stone, and replace it with a living, vibrant heart of flesh. You sacrificed your own son to make a way for me to be reconciled to you. My mind cannot fathom the breadth and depth of such love. Thank you, my Lord, for the privilege of following you.

In the Zone

Have you claimed the promise of Colossians 1:13–14? Do you believe your sins are not only covered, but washed away?

Breaking a Sweat

For physical training is of some value, but godliness has
value for all things, holding promise for both the present life
and the life to come. (1 Timothy 4:8)

As I approached my forties, the ol' metabolism began to slow a teensy
bit. The girl who could inhale a box of doughnuts in one sitting, without
receiving red-light notification from the bathroom scale, began to physically
expand. As I neared my fifties, my metabolic rate slammed on brakes so
hard I faceplanted into the steering wheel.

Something had to be done.

With fear and trembling, I purchased a gym membership. Surely the
stress of entering this intimidating new world would burn a few calories—
and help me drop a size or two.

My first day of orientation into the world of medieval torture, I
expended more calories trying to understand how the equipment worked,
than actually using it. I smiled and nodded and gave the trainer my
undivided attention, convinced I would be *that woman* who had to study
the little graphics on the side of each apparatus and would harsh everyone's
mellow by impeding gym traffic flow.

Left alone, I got busy. This would be a good thing. As casually as
possible, I studied the instructions, and used my peripheral vision to watch
the roomful of young, fit bodies in their adorable outfits. If I could achieve
even a touch of that kind of fitness, my sweetheart might consider renewing
our marriage vows. Hmm.

Then I noticed a woman across the room. She looked out of place and
unsure of herself. Her workout clothes might have been cute and trendy a
few decades ago, but they shone in stark contrast to the apparel of the tiny

fashionistas around the room. As she struggled, I felt a touch of sympathy. *Bless her heart.*

Then my vision focused. Oh, my word. *Is that a wall of mirrors?*

I slunk back to my car and headed for the nearest department store. Bless her heart, indeed.

On the next visit, I was ready. Adorned in the coolest workout gear ever, I pushed and pulled, lifted and twisted. Three repetitions here and five or six repetitions there. I was an exercise maniac. Tiny beads of sweat popped out on my upper lip.

Hmm. I should pace myself and not overdo on my first full day. I glanced at the clock.

I'd been sweating for five minutes.

After the first week of my "here and there" routine, I realized my well-intentioned approach to exercise wasn't going to change my physical condition for the better. Dabbling in a healthy lifestyle would never lead to the lasting changes I needed for overall health. I needed to get serious and tap into muscles I'd only read about in high school science class. Intense, sweat-it-out, down and dirty effort was required.

What a mirror image of our spiritual lives.

How easy for us to dabble in prayer, Bible reading, and corporate worship, skimming the surface of a life of faith. Then the inevitable storms descend, and we wonder why our roots don't hold against relentless battering. Stunned, we cry out to God whom we feel has abandoned us. *But Lord, I serve you. Why is this happening?*

If we competed in a marathon without the proper training, we would drop from fatigue in the first mile or two. Without consistent physical conditioning, we are assured of failure.

So why do we attempt to stand under life's long-distance run with the strength of rarely used spiritual muscle? Why do we pray-on-the-go and wonder why we don't hear that still small voice?

God's Word is rich with stories of men and women who moved beyond a shallow faith-life into a deep, abiding, soul-strengthening relationship with their Creator. Then, when faced with the unimaginable, they stood poised—ready for battle.

As Esther stood before her husband-king to intercede for the lives of the Jewish people, she didn't rely on a wisp of a prayer. Through fasting and the relentless seeking of God's heart, her soul was fortified with strength and wisdom. Esther 4:16 reads, "Go, gather together all the Jews who are in Susa, and fast for me. Do not eat or drink for three days, night or day. I and my attendants will fast as you do. When this is done, I will go to the king, even though it is against the law. And if I perish, I perish."

These are the actions of a woman accustomed to regular communion with God. Her roots, her *anchor* was deep, and when she witnessed storm clouds gathering, she relied on her spiritual exercise routine—time with the source of all wisdom.

We are called today to live lives of strength and honor—to glorify God in every season. Like Esther, God placed each of us in a time and location of his choosing, for a unique purpose. Our responsibility is to stay soul-fit and eager to hear his voice.

Physical fitness requires time, commitment, and grit—even more so to keep our seasoned metabolism in gear. There is value in caring for the body God gave us and in staying fit for service through the decades.

Spiritual fitness requires the same focus, plus reliance on the Holy Spirit for wisdom, guidance, strength, and perseverance. And the best part? The benefits of soul-investment reach into eternity.

Abba, Father, how I long to know you! To move beyond shallow, counterfeit living and to live a life of texture, depth, and meaning. I want my heart to be firmly tied to yours so that I think and move with your vision and wisdom. Oh, how I praise you!

In the Zone

Make note of time spent before the Lord in prayer over the last few days. Is there a pattern of praying-on-the-go? Are there intentional times of being still and quiet before the Creator? Pray, asking God to teach you and to draw you into deeper fellowship with him. Record and meditate on Scripture the Holy Spirit brings to mind in these moments.

Poised for Greatness

The King will reply, 'Truly I tell you, whatever you did for one of the least of these brothers and sisters of mine, you did for me.' (Matthew 25:40)

Her gaze held a cloudy mixture of confusion, sorrow, and frustration as she leveled a challenge toward her friends. As tears threatened, she spoke with an edge of bitterness.

"It's just not fair. I worked hard to be able to retire early and to serve in ways I've always dreamed about. I told God I would go and do whatever he wanted, *wherever* he wanted. My name was the first one on the list for an upcoming international mission trip. I've trained. I've studied. I have a *passport*, for crying out loud. And now, *this* happens."

Her friends edged closer, genuine concern defining their expressions. The woman's voice caught on a sob as she continued to unleash a steady stream of disappointment.

"I just heard that my mother needs surgery that requires a long hospital stay and months of full-time care. There is no one available to care for her. No one. Just me. Me! How could God let this happen? I thought he was calling me to do something *great* for him!"

The women's collective intake of breath was palpable as their friend's angst laid bare before them. In an instant, they could see the truth beyond her finite vision.

God *had* called her to something great. He equipped, enabled, and prepared her to be his hands and feet—the instrument of love and care—to her own mother.

Oh, how often we inform God of the clever and unique ways we will serve him. Surely, he will be impressed with our dreams and ideas of reaching the masses with the gospel. But what if our Lord calls us to the "little things"? What if our greatest acts of service don't involve exotic locations or glamorous settings?

What if our "go ye therefore" means going next door, or to the local nursing home, or to our parent's home? If God opens a door of service, who are we to say we prefer a more exciting, *prettier* door?

In 1 Samuel 12, the aging prophet Samuel speaks candidly to the nation of Israel and urges them to seek God wholeheartedly. Towards the end of his address, he says, "But be sure to fear the LORD and serve him faithfully with all your heart; consider what great things he has done for you" (v. 24).

His words must have echoed in the hearts of the people—*fear the LORD and serve him faithfully.* He reminded them God had demonstrated forgiveness, compassion, and grace. Now, the prophet called them to a life of faithful, sold-out loyalty. A life of respect and service.

Samuel then speaks of "great things" in a context that is foreign in our present, self-obsessed culture. He encourages the Israelites to consider the great things of God—how they were delivered time and again from oppression. How God forgave their disobedience and rescued them from their enemies.

"Great things" is not about us—our service, our works.

"Great things" describes the amazing, miraculous works of the Savior on our behalf.

Our claim to greatness lies in who we know and to whom we belong—Jesus, our Savior, anchor, and friend.

Through prayer and wise counsel, those who yearn to serve the Lord with greatness can commit to a life of surrender and submission. We can allow the Holy Spirit to work in our hearts—softening rough edges of selfishness and disobedience.

And we can praise the God of new things for the wondrous ways he continues to move, and for inviting us to join him in his work.

Father, please forgive my selfishness—for those times I serve with impure motives. May the purpose of my service be to declare your name and glory, not my own. I love you, Lord. Open my eyes to opportunities to declare your greatness.

In the Zone

Meditate on 1 Samuel 12:24 and Psalm 119:36. Pray, asking God to reveal any motives for service that are not of him.

Super Girl

That is why, for Christ's sake, I delight in weaknesses, in insults, in hardships, in persecutions, in difficulties. For when I am weak, then I am strong. (2 Corinthians 12:10)

The late spring day was a touch of southern magic—breezy and sun-drenched—as I corralled the twenty-plus sixth and seventh grade girls onto the physical education field. While working part-time at my daughter's school, I loved these afternoons with middle-school girls. And since the school year was winding down, today would be more relaxed with less formal activity.

I like to teach the digital generation games from the past—the "good old days." So, armed with two long ropes, I placed them parallel on the ground for a game of Jump the River. After each student "jumped the river," the river widened for the next round. If a girl's foot touched the river's rope-boundary, that person was "out."

As I cheered the girls' jumps, I enjoyed golden-hued memories of playing the game with my friends in elementary and middle school. The sounds of my students' squeals and laughter sweetened the day and confirmed the choice to be outside with old-fashioned fun.

The moment I had "The Idea" is forever ingrained in my silly, middle-aged brain. I remember kneeling beside the ropes. Teasing the girls. Soaking in the perfect, balmy day. *I can do this. I know I can! I'll get in line with the girls and jump the river. We'll call it Throw-Back Thursday. Yeah, let's do it.*

Now, in the interest of full disclosure, it wasn't unusual for this teacher to participate in student activity. I enjoyed being the pitcher in softball games and joining in rounds of "knock-out" on the basketball court. I taught tag-football basics and kickball was my forte.

But it had been awhile since I'd taken a running leap over a river—real or imagined.

In dramatic fashion, I stood and stretched to begin my run to the river. Myriad preteen girls giggled and made jokes. The afternoon breeze ruffled my hair as the wide blue yonder beckoned. I lowered my head and sprinted forward.

In retrospect, the river looked a tad wider from the air than from ground zero. But as I ballerina-leaped to clear the imaginary body of water, I felt a major rush of adrenaline. *Oh, I've so got this.*

A microsecond later I entered one of those out-of-body experiences we've all read about.

My right foot planted and absorbed the full impact of the landing. In slow motion, part of my knee went to the right, and part of it moved left. The sight, along with a tidal wave of pain and nausea, sent me to the ground in a semi-fetal position. Of course, I must have disguised my misery pretty well, because after the first wave of agony, I crawled out of the way and the girls continued their game.

This began endless months of physical therapy, surgery, and more therapy. In one unthinking moment, I deconstructed part of my leg I had assumed would always be strong and available for use. Silly, silly me.

The experience opened my eyes to a few bits of wisdom. One, I wasn't a teenager. Not even close. Two, concerning various activities, I needed to exercise restraint. My granny would have said, "Leigh Ann, it's time to use your noggin." (Translation: *Think, girl!*)

Reality is tough to accept. I think it's a pride thing. There's a serious disconnect between what my spirit thinks I *can* do and what my body knows I *can't* do. I mean, I ran track in high school. Why couldn't I go out and run a few miles this afternoon? It's only been a few (*cough-cough*) decades. And that a bout of vertigo rocked my world after spinning my granddaughter 'round and 'round doesn't mean a thing. It could happen to anyone.

Hmm. I'll stick with riding my bike. Surely, I can still pedal.

While caution is advised when attempting to run marathons and jump rivers, there are countless activities for us to enjoy through middle age and beyond. Tennis, kayaking, hiking, biking, bowling, golf, gardening, swimming, dancing, and walking are just a few of the possibilities. The important part is to keep moving and to try something new!

Our motivations are as varied as activity choices. Extra endurance is needed for those late nights in the bleachers cheering on our high schooler. Or we want to stay healthy to keep up with our grandchildren. Retirement may be around the corner and we hope to have energy to explore new frontiers.

The bottom line is that we want to stay fit for service in whatever capacity our Lord calls us. Proverbs 31:17 speaks to the strength of an honorable woman. "She sets about her work vigorously; her arms are strong for her tasks." Let's take this as a challenge to be our best, regardless of the inevitable changes and limitations. Besides, there's *never* a limit to how much we can love, share, and invest in others.

Um, excuse me a few minutes. One of my grandsons wants to play "policeman and bad guys." I've got to run before I get caught ...

Father God, some days I feel the effects of growing older in this fallen world. And sometimes, I feel like a young girl! Thank you for working in me and for keeping my heart and spirit fresh and strong. I love you, Father.

In the Zone

Read 1 Corinthians 6:19–20. Make a note of your physical activity over the past weeks. Is there room for improvement or for trying something new?

Extreme Makeover Midlife Edition

See, I am doing a new thing! Now it springs up; do you not perceive it? (Isaiah 43:19a)

The young couple huddled together and bounced with nervous energy. For weeks, they had waited to see the miraculous transformation of their previously ramshackle home. Visions of reclaimed barn wood and an open-concept living area whirled through their shiplap-studded minds. Their empty bank accounts testified to the fact they had laid everything on the line. For this moment. The big reveal.

After the commercial break.

Transformation—our culture is all about it. We are *fascinated* with big changes as evidenced by countless television programming hours devoted to extreme makeovers of home and body. We are smitten, mesmerized, and convinced. *Mercy, why is my home so dated? I should knock out a wall or two. Hmm, if their backyard can be transformed into a tropical oasis—in January—mine can too.*

On a visit to see family (*cough, cough,* two of my grandchildren) in the great state of Texas, I couldn't wait to check out a little place called Waco. I wanted to see the hometown of the dynamic duo of home transformations—Chip and Joanna Gaines. I knew that television could make places and events larger than life, so I wasn't sure what to expect from the magnolia-inspired empire.

I must say, Waco, Texas, delivered. The town and its people welcome and charm their guests. We explored the Magnolia House store, walked the grounds, admired the cute little bakery, and even bought a T-shirt. I was tempted to purchase a sprig of cotton for decorating purposes, but we have entire fields of the white fluff in North Carolina, and I didn't want to get carried away.

The Gaines family, and others like them, are uniquely gifted to see what most of us don't—they see potential. They look at old, broken-down structures and see beautiful homes. They look past the present condition and see what *could be*. Quite impressive.

But while home makeovers are fun to watch, witnessing the transformation of a human heart will take our breath away. Bitterness becomes joy and compassion. Hatred crumbles into a million pieces and is replaced by love, humility, and empathy.

We serve a God who looks past our cracks, rough edges, and our brokenness, and sees the beauty waiting to be discovered. He sees us as we were created to be—image bearers of his Son—women of life, strength, and purpose. Jeremiah 29:11 reads, "For I know the plans I have for you," declares the LORD, "plans to prosper you and not to harm you, plans to give you hope and a future." Oh, how I love this verse! Each word and phrase reverberate with expectation.

Plans. Hope. Future. Amazing, life-giving words. Words not contingent on our age or season of life. Words that don't become null and void when our children leave home, or the lines around our eyes grow deeper.

If we know Jesus as Savior, God looks at us and sees—not the peeling paint or the shaky foundation—but the righteousness of his Son. He sees us with the eyes and heart of pure, unconditional love. He sees promise and *potential*—a growing beauty who through her own metamorphosis, can influence her world for Christ.

In any renovation, there is work involved. The old must be scraped and sanded to allow for a fresh covering. Likewise, living a life of extreme change is about surrender and obedience—denying self and longing for the God of new things.

Because a woman on fire for the Lord can impact her home, her neighborhood, her workplace, and her culture.

Let's breathe in the life-giving, life-changing work of the Holy Spirit. And exhale it to our world.

Father, thank you for your ongoing work of transforming my messiness into something beautiful and for infusing my life with hope and purpose. May my joy overflow and make an eternal difference in your kingdom.

In the Zone

Are there cracks and rough edges in your heart that you long to release to the power of the Holy Spirit? Pray, asking God to renew and restore you from the inside out and to continue his transformation in you.

What About Grace?

For it is by grace you have been saved, through faith—and this is not from yourselves, it is the gift of God. (Ephesians 2:8)

Caroline was a woman on a mission—busy, driven, and not given to downtime or moments of solitude. If something needed to be done, she was the go-to girl. She led multiple committees, joined every mission trip, and volunteered at the hint of a whispered need.

Anne stood before the church activity sign-up sheets and fluttered her pen between two fingers. A friend asked if she felt the Holy Spirit's nudge to be a part of a particular opportunity. Her answer? "No, but I feel like I should. I haven't done anything in a while."

These precious, well-intentioned saints were in danger of being mired in spiritual quicksand—searching for fulfillment in activity. Each bordered on living by a spiritual checklist, trying to work their way into pleasing God and into easing a sense of emptiness.

And they were exhausted.

I recognized the signs because I'd been there. From the time I was a girl, I knew I was saved by faith, not by works. But there was a tiny place of insecurity that worried about *keeping* God's favor. My internal dialogue was a constant drain on my fragile peace.

What have you done this week? Have you visited the nursing home? Should you sign up for that Bible study? You haven't chaperoned the youth lately. You need to check on the shut-ins. Take a day to spend with friends? Do you deserve it?

I lived in a state of restlessness. Acts of service became a quick fix, easing the itch for a few days or weeks until the false guilt and worry returned.

My life exuded busyness, stress, and anxiousness—not the steady peace of Christ.

I'm convinced our checklist mentality is rooted in our desire to be loved unconditionally. As women, isn't that what we long for? To be loved and cherished no matter what? To know someone thinks we have intrinsic beauty, value, and worth?

As children, we learn if we do the right things, we receive a smile. If we do the wrong things, we are met with a frown of displeasure. We develop a craving for the approval of those around us and we'll do anything to keep that smile on others' faces.

The problem? That insatiable hunger for approval can translate to our relationship with Christ. We know him as Savior, but we still feel compelled to jump through hoops to *keep* his favor. What a debilitating way to live!

But there is good news—amazing, mind-blowing news. We don't have to work from a checklist. We have his favor. Our God is the *author* of unconditional love. For those of us who struggle with acceptance and approval, Romans 5:8 is rich with hope. "But God demonstrates his own love for us in this: While we were still sinners, Christ died for us."

When did God show his great love for us? After we completed various acts of service? After we turned in our spiritual checklists? After we took a shower and dressed in our Sunday best?

He demonstrated pure, absolute love, *while we were still sinners.* Christ's sacrifice on our behalf was based on his love—not on anything we had done or ever will do. We didn't earn, purchase, or deserve his favor. Our salvation was a gift.

The gift of grace.

Breathe in the beauty of Romans 8:38–39—"For I am convinced that neither death nor life, neither angels nor demons, neither the present nor the future, nor any powers, neither height nor depth, nor anything else in all creation, will be able to separate us from the love of God that is in Christ Jesus our Lord."

When we grab hold of this treasure and absorb this truth into each corner of our hearts and minds—that nothing can separate us from the love of God—something incredible takes place. Something quickens inside the muddy depths of our doubts and insecurities.

We experience a crazy freedom, a hope-filled giddiness that bubbles over into joy. In a strange and marvelous working of the Holy Spirit, we are then *compelled* to engage in acts of service because we're eager to express love for our Savior and Lord.

The difference? Instead of serving to earn brownie points or to retain favor, we serve as an act of worship—to show love and adoration to the One who made us for his glory. Service becomes relational, us and God on mission together.

We long for our children to call, text, or visit out of love, not because they think we're keeping a tally on them. We yearn for relationship, not time given out of a sense of duty. Likewise, we were created for a dynamic faith-walk with our heavenly Father—a journey overflowing with love and devotion, not enslaved by a sense of obligation.

Our dog-eared checklists serve no purpose, other than to create lives of stress and frustration. The time is now to break free from the shackles of a works-based faith and to discover peace and rest in the unconditional love of the Father.

Because it's all about grace—beautiful, unmerited, *grace.*

Oh, Lord, I long for genuine relationship with you—to serve from a heart of love and gratitude—not from a draining sense of duty. Help me to rest in the depths of your unconditional love and acceptance and to embrace your priceless gift of grace. I love you, Father. Thank you.

In the Zone

Review your recent acts of service. Was there an awareness of joy and thankfulness in these activities? Meditate on Psalm 36:7. How does God want to change your attitudes toward ministry?

Clearing the Clutter

Be kind and compassionate to one another, forgiving each other, just as in Christ God forgave you. (Ephesians 4:32)

There is a place where the only natural light is a tiny shaft streaking through an outer air vent, illuminating dust particles as they perform a chaotic dance. A place of dark corners and ghostly shapes. A place of unbearable heat one day, and finger-numbing cold in another.

A place we pretend doesn't exist when company comes a' calling.

Oh, we know it's there—in some back alley of our minds. We have every intention of going there someday. To fix things. The thought brings a shudder, but what if the Lord moved us to our home in glory and someone entered our earthly homes and discovered *the place*?

Let's take a deep breath and enter this place together. You know, *the attic*.

(Cue scary music.)

For most of us, the attic (or basement or hall closet) isn't a simple stroll down memory lane, it's a catapult through time and space. We soar through millions of memories and land with a heart-skipping thud. *What happened? How did I get here?*

We push through boxes of baby clothes, school report cards, and little league trophies. A ridiculous stack of old textbooks gather dust in a corner. Board games and puzzles with missing pieces compete for space with once-loved stuffed animals and Matchbox cars. We drag an old stool through the labyrinth of disorder and attempt to make sense of the mess. That's when we notice the photos. And something called *negatives*.

Three hours later, we've laughed, cried, and relived a lifetime. And we haven't made a dent in our attic overhaul.

What a unique time of life. We've lived a little—the evidence surrounds us. Our minds skim through countless recitals, concerts, and ballgames. Our thoughts rest briefly on visits to the emergency room and midnight fever spikes. We remember kisses and arguments, hugs and tears. Our wistful musings are filled with sadness—and joy, and *thanksgiving*.

And we pause in wonder of how we can experience such varied emotions in the same breath.

Time to enjoy mementoes from the past is a unique gift. I've never heard anyone express regret over saving special things from their years of raising a family. But I have heard regrets of mismanaging clutter and decades of debris.

There is a time to let stuff *go*. There is physical and emotional freedom in the declutter process. Not to mention, extra space.

The same is true of the corners and closed-off rooms of our hearts. Over the years, we may cling to dust and clutter at the expense of our inner spirit—that mysterious place our Creator wants to nurture and grow in his likeness. We fool ourselves into complacency. *No one can see that back corner stacked with grudges and unforgiveness. Nobody is hurt by my ... stuff.*

It's time for a mirror-moment. Bravery is required, but the benefits are immense. Let's grab a stool and sort through the mess. Over the years, have we kept a running tally on anyone? Has any bitterness taken root in our hearts?

We are tempted to defend and rationalize our hoarding. *But you don't understand. This person hurt and betrayed me and my family. They were cruel and unthinking. In fact, this person has never even apologized for hurting me. I have every right to keep that stack of resentment in the back of the closet.*

God's word stands resolute at the edge of our subconscious. We hear truth as from a great distance. "If you, LORD, kept a record of sins, Lord, who could stand? But with you there is forgiveness, so that we can, with reverence, serve you" (Psalm 130:3–4).

Our fighting and rationalizations seem absurd. Who could possibly stand under the weight of every unforgiven sin? Who could bear the weight?

Still, we point and shake our fingers. Lord, they ...

His word echoes through us. *Who could stand? Who could stand? Who could stand?*

We are faced with another question. Did Jesus die for everyone—except for that one person who drives us crazy or hurt us so deeply?

Unforgiveness goes beyond a little dust—it's more like that gunk on the sides of the oven, or the mold that grows in damp places and causes damage to every breath we take. If it stays in the shadows, unforgiveness will defeat us.

But what if we continue to expose that bitter root to the light of God's Word?

Galatians 6:1 reads "Brothers and sisters, if someone is caught in a sin, you who live by the Spirit should restore that person gently. But watch yourselves, or you also may be tempted." Oh, how the beautiful phrase, *restore that person gently,* should call to us. Forgiveness brings healing and restoration—to the offender and to the one offended.

And restoration brings freedom. Freedom to live, love, and serve the one who makes this fresh beginning possible.

Is forgiving difficult? Was it difficult for Jesus to offer us a clean start? Did it cost him anything? Did he offer it with a closed fist, or an open hand?

Do we truly want to be free from the gunk and mold and heart-clutter of unforgiveness? Through the power of the Holy Spirit, are we ready to scrape it clean and toss it out?

Oh, Father, please do a clean-sweep of my heart! Shine light in the hidden places and chase away every shadow of resentment, anger, or bitterness. I want to be free to serve without hindrance—to love with pure, unencumbered motives. Thank you, Lord, for fresh beginnings.

In the Zone

Pray over Psalm 139:23–24, asking God to reveal any hidden areas of resentment and unforgiveness. Praise him for his patience and lovingkindness.

Broken and Beautiful

But we have this treasure in jars of clay to show that this all-surpassing power is from God and not from us. (2 Corinthians 4:7)

Sara was a fraud—or so she thought. A faithful member of the church, she stayed involved in myriad activities, willing to offer support when needed. In her mid-fifties, she served with the enthusiasm and energy of someone half her age.

But no one really knew Sara beyond her eagerness to help. She never shared her life beyond small talk or talked of spiritual things deeper than surface level. She came, she served, she left. And she exuded an underlying sense of *something*.

Our churches are full of Saras. Precious women with scarred pasts who assume they are unworthy and unqualified to be used of God in a powerful way. Women who define themselves by their regrets and failures. *I've done this, and I'll always be defined by it. God could never use me because of my past.* They may stay busy, but their hearts never engage. A wall is erected to keep the secrets hidden and to prevent others from gaining access.

Oh, what an isolated, lonely life of faith.

A familiar Scripture, but one difficult to apply to ourselves, is 1 John 1:9. "If we confess our sins, he is faithful and just and will forgive us our sins and purify us from all unrighteousness." We will look someone in the eyes and tell them they are forgiven by a loving God. We will encourage them to live lives of purity and freedom because they are justified by faith.

But when it comes to our personal failures and mistakes, we don't quite believe the hype. *How could God forgive that?*

I believe there's a fatal flaw in those of us who own a bit of real estate in the pew each Sunday morning. We paste on a smile and act like a Mary, when we *feel* like a Rahab.

I mean, everyone knows that Marys are holy and pure and have it all together. They teach Sunday school, go on mission trips, and have amazing children. Their marriages are strong—filled with fun, laughter, and closeness. They have cute clothes, a cute smile, and a cute life. *Bleh.*

But Rahab? Wasn't she the, um, harlot? She was flawed and faithless. How can you even hint we might feel like a Rahab?

Because, like Rahab, we are sinners in need of a Savior. And because I've been there, and maybe, you have too. Underneath the Sunday morning smile, we've felt unworthy, unfit, and undeserving. And we've kept our hearts closed off for fear of being found out.

Let's focus the light of God's Word on this area of insecurity. This pit of regret and failure is deep and dark and can be like living with a vise around our souls—choking off a life of abundant, joyful living. If unworthiness is a personal struggle, take a breath and get excited. Because God's got this covered.

Hebrews chapter eleven is often called the faith chapter, or the faith hall of fame. Biblical giants of honor and holy service fill each verse. Men like Abel, Enoch, Noah, and Abraham. Also, Isaac, Jacob, Joseph, and Moses. And the women? Let's see, how many are listed? Although there are many examples of faithful females in Scripture, only two are mentioned in this passage of the hallowed hall of faith. Sarah, the wife of Abraham, and ... Rahab.

"By faith the prostitute Rahab, because she welcomed the spies, was not killed with those who were disobedient" (v. 31).

The writer of Hebrews then gets so excited with his list of faithful servants, he confides his lack of time to write about each one in detail.

"And what more shall I say? I do not have time to tell about Gideon, Barak, Samson and Jephthah, about David and Samuel and the prophets, who through faith conquered kingdoms, administered justice, and gained what was promised; who shut the mouths of lions, quenched the fury of the flames, and escaped the edge of the sword; whose weakness was turned to strength; and who became powerful in battle and routed foreign armies" (vv. 32–34).

Through faith, these men and women conquered kingdoms, shut the mouths of lions, quenched flames, escaped the sword, welcomed spies—and risked their very lives out of faith in the one true God. And my favorite part? Because of their faith, these were servants *whose weakness was turned to strength.*

Their weakness turned to strength and they became powerful in battle.

This is amazing. Someone as flawed and *sinful* as Rahab gets an honorable mention in the hall of faith. Wait for it—the news gets even better. Rahab is in the family line of Jesus. Boaz called her "mom." King David called her "great-great-grandma."

Everyone mentioned in the hall of faith was a less-than-perfect individual. But God still used them to accomplish his purposes.

Are we ready to take our tattered lists of regrets and failures and toss them out? To open every corner of our hearts to the healing light of God's word? The time is now to stand on the foundation of Christ's unconditional love and to accept the forgiveness and restoration our Lord died to give us.

Place your hand in the Father's. Let him take your weaknesses and transform them into strengths—ready for love, service, and battle.

Oh, dear one. Now is the time.

Abba, Father, I am so weary of living with this weight of regrets and mess-ups. They suffocate me and crush my joy. Your word says you love me. That your love conquers my hateful past and gives me an inheritance of hope. Oh, help me, dear Lord! Empower me to stand with confidence on your love and to accept the forgiveness and tender beginning you provided on the cross. Thank you, Father. I love you.

In the Zone

Read the fascinating account of Rahab's faith-in-action in Joshua 2:1–21. Take note of her confident declaration in verse 11 and her action in verse 21. Write your own declaration of faith in Christ, then pray, asking for the assurance to trust in his promises of restoration.

Playing the Game

Each one should test their own actions. Then they can take pride in themselves alone, without comparing themselves to someone else, for each one should carry their own load. (Galatians 6:4–5)

The day was long and exhausting, and we're ready for some grab-the-pajama-pants downtime. We think about taking a walk, but, well, maybe tomorrow. With our favorite snack on standby, we pop open the laptop or cellphone, and go surfing instead. Yeah. Surfing. A little easier on the joints.

We scroll by posts and images of puppies doing silly things, someone's new piercing, and a we-don't-dare-answer-back political rant. Our stomachs growl as we salivate over a calorie-free triple-chocolate-cake recipe on the newsfeed. *Hmm, calorie free? I do need to lose a few pounds.* Someone wants us to like their professional page. So-and-so is donating their birthday to charity. We weren't planning on giving a gift, but ...

Once in a while, there's a prayer request. *Oh, I didn't know that. Of course, I'll pray.*

For a moment, we enjoy a touch of contentment—a feeling of community. Being part of a virtual world where we *like* and comment on each other's lives is *fun*. There's a sense of belonging when we're "in the know."

Then it happens. Friends post photos of their exotic vacation on a remote Caribbean island. Someone shares memories of their once-in-a-lifetime excursion floating down the Mississippi river—in a kayak. Our jaws drop at family portraits taken in a field—beside a barn—with late afternoon sunlight highlighting smiling parents with adorable children. You-know-who posts before and after shots of her forty-pound weight loss. We see a couple the same age as we are enjoying hotdogs and popcorn at their grandchildren's baseball game. Wearing a T-shirt reading *World's Best Nana*.

Everyone's life seems bigger, sweeter, and more packed with adventure. Many enjoy a heart full of grandbabies, and we wonder if that magic will ever happen to us.

That long-ago decision to stay home with the kiddos a few years is starting to bite. Our peers with double-incomes are enjoying homes at the beach and more travel opportunities. Their careers are soaring, and a few even contemplate early retirement. *Really?*

Our gaze shifts to the snack bowl and comfy pants. *What am I doing with my life?*

In an instant, our snacks lose appeal. We aren't quite so hungry anymore because we've been feeding on something with an aftertaste. A touch of envy takes root as we play another round of a familiar game we don't enjoy. Because we never win.

The stacked-against-us game of comparison.

Oh, the dangers of comparing our ordinary days with others' highlight reels! Because they *are* highlights. Snapshots of moments in time when smiles are bright, and garments are clean. No one is bickering or throwing a tantrum. And have you noticed? No one shares photos of late nights paying the bills or 3 a.m. prayers begging God to take the migraine away. We watch each other live in one dimension—no fuss, no mess.

But life *is* messy. And when we play this soul-shrinking game, we lose, lose, lose. When Theodore Roosevelt said, "Comparison is the thief of joy,"[2] he was sharing God-given wisdom. He knew that contentment morphs into an unattainable dream dependent on *someday when. Someday when my life looks like theirs, I'll be happy.*

God's word is clear on the subject. "A heart at peace gives life to the body, but envy rots the bones" (Proverbs 14:30). Wow. Rots the bones? That's rather, um, disgusting. But isn't that how we feel when the weeds of jealousy threaten to choke our fragile contentment? Inadequate and *disgusting?*

Mark 12:30 provides a healthier option. "Love the Lord your God with all your heart and with all your soul and with all your mind and with all your strength." And 1 Timothy 6:6–8 reads, "But godliness with contentment is great gain. For we brought nothing into the world, and we can take nothing out of it. But if we have food and clothing, we will be content with that."

With God's strength, we can make the choice to *not* play the game. We can enjoy and celebrate the successes of others and maintain a Christ-centered perspective. We can live 1 Thessalonians 5:18—"Give thanks in all circumstances; for this is God's will for you in Christ Jesus."

Author Beth Moore has said, "All that will matter in eternity is the glory that came to God as a result of my life. I will be most blessed when God is most glorified."[3]

When this is our heart—regardless of our neighbors' triumphs—our envy melts before it even begins to harden.

We can count blessings. Give thanks. Trust God to work all for our good.

And we can be content with that.

Lord, when I'm tempted to harbor envy in my heart, help me to maintain an eternal perspective. I long to truly rejoice in the joys of others and to express genuine compassion in their disappointments. Convict me to give thanks and to be content in my moments. Thank you, Jesus.

In the Zone

Ask God to search your heart for evidence of discontentment. In an attitude of prayer, ask these questions: Is my lack of contentment based on the successes of others? Have I fallen into a pattern of envy-based comparison? Meditate on 1 Timothy 6:6–8 and lay your struggles at Jesus's feet. In the coming days, take note of the seeds of joy that have been allowed to grow by removing the weeds of resentment.

Unexpected Benefits

You make known to me the path of life; you will fill me with joy in your presence, with eternal pleasures at your right hand. (Psalm 16:11)

The moment was rather strange. A few days before, we helped our baby girl settle in at college and now, were experiencing a Sunday service with just the two of us. Knowing an empty house awaited us, emotions ran high as we lingered after the service and watched the blur of activity. Families gathered in groups and made plans for lunch. Little ones roamed and darted around the legs of parents and church family. Teenagers huddled in groups and discussed the latest ballgame and a movie they wanted to see. A little stunned with the events of the last few days, we took the sights all in and wondered, *What just happened?*

We knew adjusting to the life changes before us would take time, but we were caught off guard by this particular moment. As families trickled away to their afternoon activities, my sweetheart and I looked at each other and blinked. I believe he was the first to speak. "What would you like for lunch, my bride?" (I love when he calls me that.)

As we stood contemplating the day before us, the slow smile hijacking my face seemed a replica of my husband's. We could go anywhere. We could hit any restaurant. We could even go *out of town* if we so desired. We could check out one of those grown-up eateries with soft music in the background and nice tablecloths. Or we could pick up something and take it home.

A touch giddy with the endless possibilities, we worked to keep from racing to the car. *That's it, stay composed. Don't look too excited.*

This is a time of change, but also one of discovery. For years, we have lived by an endless schedule filled with appointments, practices, recitals, and ballgames. Every waking thought revolved around, *what's next? Who needs to be where today?*

The temptation is strong to become mired in the past—to grieve all that's changed. To spend our days reliving a home full of noise and busyness and longing for the used-to-be. My friend, Connie, has the ability to look in my eyes and know within seconds if I'm emotionally stuck in the past. She also has a wise phrase she'll share to snap me out of it.

"Don't park there."

Ride by the memories, give a wave, and a prayer of thanks. But don't put the car in park. Don't stay and let the engine be flooded by the endless pumping of visions of yesteryear. Refuse to be crippled by gripping the past so fiercely our fingers turn blue.

Release and *live*. Release and *grow*. Release and *discover*.

The possibilities are even bigger and brighter than enjoying a grown-up restaurant. Think back to the before-children era. What did we enjoy? What hobbies did we lay aside to raise a family? What dreams have lain dormant, waiting for something called *extra time*? Are there places we'd love to visit that don't revolve around arcades and kiddie pools?

Once upon a time, were we crafty? Do we long to pick up a paint brush, compose a story on the laptop, or remodel a spare bedroom? Maybe we need to update a skill set by taking an online class or exploring the campus of the local community college. Have we put off joining that mission group or Bible study? How can we be the *me* God created us to be in the here and now?

In all the inevitable changes, one thing stands firm—our Lord's plans and purposes for us. Romans 11:29 overflows with excitement and hope. "For God's gifts and his call are irrevocable." The way God wired us, with unique gifts, interests, and passions, is meant to be of life-long use. Now, we may have a few extra minutes to devote in nurturing that uniqueness.

This is also a time to cheer each other on—to encourage one another to keep running the race God has given us. When our friend rejoins the choir after years away, give a thumbs-up and a hug. When someone walks into our women's group after being absent awhile, show a smile of welcome and a heart of grace.

One of God's greatest benefits on this journey of change and discovery, is the joy of knowing we're not alone. As we take a new step in the strength of our Lord, we can look on each side of us, and take the hand of a fellow traveler.

So, let's have a goal-setting heart to heart with our sweethearts. Let's get the girlfriends together for coffee. We have benefits to explore!

Father, I'm beginning to feel the stirrings of excitement and new possibilities. Guide me as I seek to discover new paths of opportunity and more ways to bring glory to you. Thank you, Lord, that I'm never alone.

In the Zone

Make a list of your unique gifts and abilities. If stumped, ask a trusted friend for their insights. Ask God how he wants to use your uniqueness to reach others in his name.

Hot Mess

Therefore, with minds that are alert and fully sober, set your hope on the grace to be brought to you when Jesus Christ is revealed at his coming. (1 Peter 1:13)

The realization I had entered the midlife zone hit like a rogue tidal wave as we prepared to give our oldest daughter away in marriage. Talk about illogical. Why would we want to *give away* one of our greatest treasures? How could one of our babies be getting married? Why, just yesterday, three sweet bodies each claimed a stool at the kitchen counter as we prepared for a quick supper before dashing out the door for another activity. Surely, we could be a young family of five a little while longer. Could we, um, stop this infernal clock?

For Wendy, the changing season crept in unnoticed, until she found herself strapped into the seat of a physical and emotional roller coaster of monster-like proportions. On the foggy days, she fought tears and bouts of illogical worry. Her body was on fire, and the battle against weight gain was going to the enemy. This precious mom—who called herself a hot mess—wondered where her life was going and if she was being the woman God called her to be.

In times of focus and clarity, Wendy experienced a spark of excitement about the days to come. Without the responsibilities of full-time parenting, she hoped to enjoy quality time with the hubby and to explore their someday-when dreams of travel. Her heart swelled with joy as she watched her daughters take bold steps into the future, and she cherished the opportunity to lead their cheering sections.

In her relationship with God, Wendy longed for a greater depth of intimacy. She knew where her strength was anchored, and her heart reached for her Savior. But even in her longing, it was difficult to still and quiet her soul while struggling with volatile emotions.

Paula's introduction to the middle years was more of a vague feeling. Physical changes tiptoed in, including new aches and pains, flashes of heat, random strands of gray, and newly discovered wrinkles. Her son entering high school was a reminder that the days of full-time parenting grew short. "We only have about four more years with (our son) before he goes away to school. Our time together is precious, so we have made a conscious decision to *not* commit to anything unless it is of utmost importance."

But while many changes require adjustment, Paula is optimistic about the path ahead. She and her husband love trying new things and are excited about the next stage of their lives. She is also more aware of God's work in her life. "I find my focus is more on spiritual things and things of God, more so than ever in my life."

In this strange and wonderful season, as we fluctuate between anxiety and exhilaration, we can take joy in knowing God will continue to comfort, guide, and use us. We may be a super-hot mess but we're never too messy for an all-powerful God.

But how do we find that place of rest and stability? How *do* we still and quiet our souls?

Blessings await when we take intentional steps to slow our pace and to savor each moment. It seems counterintuitive, but the yearning for stillness needs to lead to the *action* of being still. Ask any five-year-old—it takes effort to stop moving!

Psalm 62:5 reads, "Yes, my soul, find rest in God; my hope comes from him." We desire soul-rest. We maintain a desperate search for it. But the Scripture is clear—our rest and our hope come from him. Not random, fleeting thoughts of him, but quiet moments of communion with the one who know us to every joint and fiber.

I love Psalm 119:36–37. "Turn my heart toward your statutes and not toward selfish gain. Turn my eyes away from worthless things; preserve my life according to your word." There is a tendency to fall into the *me* trap—*I feel yucky, I'm tired, I don't want things to change,* etc. But God calls us to turn our hearts toward him, toward his statutes. This is a purposeful shift, a deliberate change of focus that requires serious effort.

The last phrase of this verse makes me want to shout from the rooftops. *Preserve my life according to your Word.* Yes, Lord! Our lives feel off-balance.

We wonder who we are and what's next. But God will *preserve* our lives. When we turn to him, seeking him with our whole being, he will not abandon us.

He will take this hot mess and continue the transformation into something of exquisite beauty—a sold-out vessel—filled with cool, fresh, living water.

Ready to be poured out for his glory.

Father, I long to still and quiet my soul before you. Even as my outer shell is changing, I want the inside of me—the precious place where you reside—to grow more like you. May your love and likeness transform me into a useful instrument in your hands. Thank you, Father.

In the Zone

Think over the past week and note times of stillness and quiet before the Lord. How can your schedule be adjusted to allow for increased quality time with your Creator? Is there a special place where you can withdraw from the noise of each day and focus on the inner life?

The Greatest Love

For I am the LORD your God who takes hold of your right hand and says to you, Do not fear; I will help you. (Isaiah 41:13)

This wasn't how life was supposed to be. Michelle's heart ached as she and her teenage son began a six hundred-mile one-way trip covering three states. A fresh start awaited her—a new home, community, and career. But as she gripped the steering wheel and drove through unfamiliar territory, thoughts of all she was leaving behind threatened her peace and resolve.

How can I live so far away from my college girl? Did I abandon her? What about Mom and Dad? Won't they need me? How can we leave our home? Lord, what am I doing?

Michelle never expected to be a single parent in her forties. Without a spouse to share household responsibilities, the weight of every family decision pressed in on her. Each choice and evaluation—no matter how simple—appeared life-altering, and the constant stress made her vulnerable to moments of anxiety. *What if I'm doing the wrong thing?*

As we talked, Michelle's eyes filled with a watery peace as she thought back to the difficult days. "I could've been overwhelmed. I could have sunk under the weight of it all. But God reminded me that I *did* have someone. I crawled into the lap of my heavenly Father and experienced an intense friendship like no other. God pursued me and met my needs. He would never leave or forsake me."

This sweet saint had a foundation of dependence—she knew the source of her strength and hope. The moment she felt alone, she *ran* to her Lord and clung for life and breath. And in doing so, she showed her children and others around her, that she served a mighty God, indeed.

One who would never leave or forsake her. One who took her by the hand and said, *do not fear, I will help you.* The Eternal One who loved her beyond her understanding.

In a culture that shuns the virtues of loyalty, devotion, and faithfulness, the depth of love offered by Christ is considered strange and unattainable. But the words of Zephaniah 3:17 should cause our lips to sing praise and our hearts to soar. "The LORD your God is with you, the Mighty Warrior who saves. He will take great delight in you; in his love he will no longer rebuke you, but will rejoice over you with singing."

Take a moment to soak in the truth-filled words of this verse. He is with us. He will fight for us (the Mighty Warrior); he delights in us. He will *rejoice over us with singing.* Wait, really? The maker of heaven and earth will *rejoice over me* with singing?

When's the last time someone rejoiced over us? Did our parents sing over us as children? Were we serenaded during the flighty days of courtship?

Maybe it's easier to grasp this *rejoicing* when we think of how we felt when first cradling our newborns. Oh, how our hearts burst with awe and wonder! Did we weep with thankfulness? Marvel at each finger and toe? Laugh with a depth of happiness we didn't think possible?

These moments are but a shadow of how our Lord takes joy in us.

We can stand strong and true because the one who takes us by the hand is the inexhaustible source of strength and stability. When plans change, and our journeys encounter unexpected detours, we can rest in the perfect love of our Savior.

A love without measure—unconditional and enduring.

Father God, I am humbled by the depth and width of your love. I am overcome in your holy presence. Thank you for being my never-ending source of stability and strength. I praise you, dear Lord!

In the Zone

Meditate on the following verses: Deuteronomy 7:9, Psalm 136:26, and Romans 8:37–39. Praise God for his trustworthy precepts and promises. Choose one verse to write on a notecard and commit it to memory.

The Toddler Syndrome

You will keep in perfect peace those whose minds are
steadfast, because they trust in you. (Isaiah 26:3)

Join me on a quick skip down memory lane. Gaze through that portal
in time and look upon the faces of the little ones. If we don't have children,
think back to nieces and nephews, or the cherubs in the church nursery.
Oh, the sweet smiling faces. Most of the time.

Look closer. See the storm clouds brewing? Watch as sweet little faces
turn red and tears hang from delicate lashes. A tantrum builds. An adorable
volcano prepares to erupt.

Toddler emotions are more volatile than the barometric pressure in the
South. During hurricane season. But why? What is at the foundation of
such preschool angst?

Our precious babies desired their own way. Insisted on it, actually. How
many times did we hear, "I can do it by myself." With an independent
streak wider than the Mississippi, their minds were *convinced* they had a
better, wiser way. They didn't need help from anyone.

Thank goodness we outgrow the silly tendencies of our childhood
(heavy sarcasm dripping here). We all know that a grown-up with a
stubborn heart makes a toddler's attitude look like, um, child's play. While
evidence of a two-year-old's angst is clear (to all in a three-mile radius), our
inner tantrums are easier to conceal.

Until our peace crumbles from feeble attempts to do life on our own.

How often do we turn to God as a last resort in a crisis? Or when life
putters along without conflict, how tempted are we to leave our Bibles on
the bedside table collecting dust?

The neglect of God's word and time with him in prayer has to be the most neglected area in the Christian's life. We're so *busy*. Our lives are noisy, and it's hard to hear God's voice. But a steady diet of Scripture and time alone with our Lord is the cornerstone of our Christ-walk.

On some level, we know this. If asked, we would tell others the same—to read their Bibles and pray. But we *live* as if it's an optional activity. If things are fine, and we don't have a minute to take an extra breath, what's the big deal?

The "big deal" comes to light when our worlds stop their everything-is-fine spinning. When we feel sucker-punched by unwelcome circumstances. The habit of daily time with Jesus is our anchor when the storms rage. And from experience, we know the storms *will* come. If we're not in the middle of one now, there is one in our rearview mirror or on the not-so-distant horizon.

We've all been there. Times when our hearts are so full of sorrow and anguish, we can't find the words to pray. Times we are tired and battered. If we've held to God's word—tucked it in our hearts and minds—in the everyday, *ordinary* day, it will be there as our lifeline.

Oh, the moments I've fallen at the feet of Jesus with hurt and confusion so heavy the words refused to come. All I could do was think and breathe Scripture I had learned long ago, but that the Holy Spirit brought to mind in my need.

Lord, my heart is breaking. Lord, I don't know what to say. I just hurt.

I love Philippians 4:6–7 in the *Message* translation. "Don't fret or worry. Instead of worrying, pray. Let petitions and praises shape your worries into prayers, letting God know your concerns. Before you know it, a sense of God's wholeness, everything coming together for good, will come and settle you down. It's wonderful what happens when Christ displaces worry at the center of your life."

Reread the verse. *Let petitions and praises shape your worries into prayers ... a sense of God's wholeness ... Christ displaces worry at the center of your life.* Why, oh why, do we clench our fists and tell God we can handle things ourselves? Does our spiritual independence ever lead to anything but feelings of desperate exhaustion? Why do we exhaust every silly resource of this world before turning to the ultimate answer in Christ?

There's no disclaimer. I've yet to find a verse that speaks to prayer and time in the Word as being a back-up plan for when our efforts fail. Living with toddler syndrome robs us of living with victory in the One who died to make it possible. We miss out on truckloads of peace, hope, and perspective.

May our hearts long for such sweet communion with our Savior, that his tender voice fills our spirit regardless of the skies being a sun-drenched blue or darkened with shades of black and gray.

Besides, I think we'll all agree—there's nothing adorable about a midlife toddler-tantrum.

Father, I confess my hardheartedness and my tendency to insist on my own way. I yearn for deeper communion with you that I may face my days with your strength as my anchor. Thank you for your forgiveness and patience.

In the Zone

Focus on Isaiah 26:3. Ask God to reveal areas where you have been self-dependent instead of God-dependent.

A Time to Laugh

A cheerful heart is good medicine, but a crushed spirit dries
up the bones. (Proverbs 17:22)

My sweetheart and I paused in our conversation and gave each other a
befuddled stare. After a few seconds, I broke the silence with, "Um, have we
had this conversation?" We fought giggles and snickers, and admitted that
yes, indeed, we'd discussed this very topic—in detail—only days before.

Rene paused from her reading when the bed shook to the point she
couldn't maintain her place. Even with headphones and a silent computer,
her husband was lost in his own entertaining world—over a video of *The
Three Stooges*, no less. Rene rolled her gaze and in spite of her aversion to
the famous idiots, joined in the contagious laughter.

My sister, Charlene, and her husband find that seeing the silly in life
continues to enrich their marriage. To the chagrin of their children, they
like to quip, "We are as cool as tube socks and disco!"

One of the many perks of this season is the never-ending supply of
topics and situations to laugh about. I mean, really. We mid-lifers are so
funny. We "fight" over the hymnbook, one pushing, the other pulling, in
our futile attempts to see the page. We have reading glasses scattered in
every nook and corner of the house and cars, but we can't find them to save
our lives.

Standing after an extended stay on the couch elicits a dramatic moan.
After a meal, we hear the regular crunch of Tums or Rolaids. We scurry
around the house looking for "that odd noise" only to discover it's the
crackling of our knees as we walk.

But isn't it fun to laugh? To let go with a snort, giggle, or guffaw? Not at
each other—*with* each other—in hilarious communion over the absurdities

of life. Choosing to laugh adds a depth of texture and color to our days. And the shared moments bind us to each other in an us-against-the-world kind of way. What a treasure.

There's also science behind the phenomenon. Laughter relieves stress and tension, gives us a boost of oxygen-rich air, vitalizes our organs and muscles, and gets those endorphins releasing at breakneck speed. There is also research that this "good medicine" is a natural pain reliever, helps our immune system, and improves our overall mood.[4]

Chuck Swindoll was right on target when he said, "Laughter is the most beautiful and beneficial therapy God ever granted humanity."[5]

We laugh because we're made in the image of the God of joy and laughter. Luke 6:21 reminds us that the comfort to come includes the ability to laugh where previously we wept. "Blessed are you who hunger now, for you will be satisfied. Blessed are you who weep now, for you will laugh." And who can forget the giddy joy of Abraham's wife, Sarah, when God blessed them with a child in their old age. "Sarah said, 'God has brought me laughter, and everyone who hears about this will laugh with me'" (Genesis 21:6).

I love to imagine God's laughter echoing throughout the vast universe as he created each living thing. What pleasure he took in his good creation! From the world's largest Rafflesia flower in Malaysia, to the Vegetable Sheep plant in New Zealand, to the Baobab tree in Madagascar[6], our Creator is so joyfully *creative*. And that's *plant* life!

Surf the web and explore the crazy-fun animal life in our Lord's repertoire. Can you hear the divine chortles of delight? *Oh, they're going to love the camel with two humps and the platypus with the duck's bill and the otter's feet. And I can't wait for them to see the wombat, the seahorse, and the octopus!*

But wait. This gets better. In a huge burst of loving hilarity, he exercised the pinnacle of his artistic genius. From the dust, God formed creatures called *man* and *woman*, breathed into them life—and of all things—gave them a will.

Even through the sorrow before him, did he gaze through time and smile at our feeble humor? Did his heart leap as he envisioned the exquisite festivity to come? 1 Corinthians 2:9 should lead to giggles of anticipation. "However, as it is written: "What no eye has seen, what no ear has heard, and what no human mind has conceived—the things God has prepared for those who love him."

Oh, how fun to dream of our days of eternity, when the moment we think we can't laugh harder or gasp deeper in wonder, our Father God peels back another layer of joyful intensity. *Oh, child, you think that's something, look and listen to this!*

Laughter is another facet of the fathomless love of the Savior. So, go ahead. Smile bigger. Chuckle deeper. Toss back your head and laugh until it hurts. Feel the Lord's pleasure.

And know he's taking joy in ours.

Dear Father of delight and wonder, thank you for the gift of laughter. Thank you for the refreshment it brings mentally, physically, and spiritually. Give me eyes to see and ears to listen for the jewels of joy in my life. I love you, Father. Oh, how I look forward to laughing with you in glory!

In the Zone

Does it seem strange to think of God laughing with delight? Make note of opportunities to share amusement with the Lord. Tell him when you experience funny moments in the day-to-day and thank him for these unique gifts.

What Really Matters?

Never be lacking in zeal, but keep your spiritual fervor,
serving the Lord. (Romans 12:11)

There's a unique view from the middle. We look ahead and observe
our parents or older friends with a heart of appreciation and greater
understanding. Because our journeys have included the unexpected, we
begin to "get it" on the subjects of loss and sacrifice. A new maturity takes
root, and we discern that our days on this earth are truly numbered.

We turn our gaze to the past, and our eyes widen as we see the incredible
amount of time devoted to the trivial. Oh, the hours spent stressing over
appearances and what others might be thinking! We ponder the time
dedicated to the building of a life—the urgency of marriage, motherhood,
and career choices. The pursuit of stuff, from clothes to cars to gadgets. The
longing for achievement. The need to *arrive*.

This is the place. This *zone*, a crazy moment in time when we can
become frozen—unable to take the next step. And it begs the question,
*what really matters? If I'm over halfway through my time on this earth, what
have I been doing, and what needs to change?*

If we believe we are on this planet to glorify God with our hearts, souls,
and minds, then the real questions should come into focus. In the day to
day, are we being poured out as an offering? Are we living with vision and
purpose? Isn't this the bottom line in the Christian life—to live, engage,
and *breathe* the gospel of Jesus Christ?

Our forward motion may have stalled, but it's time to fire the engine,
shift gears, and get moving. We have gifts and abilities to use in Kingdom
work—and no one can take our God-ordained places. If our uniqueness
languishes on a shelf because we're too afraid to move forward, everyone

suffers—us, from stagnation, and others, from missing the benefit of our gifts.

God has placed us on a unique mission field. We are called to love and serve him where we are. Who are those we are in contact with on a regular basis? This could include a spouse, children, grandchildren, extended family, neighbors, a best friend, a boss, coworkers, our customers, clients, the cashier at the grocery store, the waitstaff at our favorite restaurant, the one who delivers our mail or paper, or the precious soul who pours our coffee at Starbucks or McDonalds.

From the time our feet hit the floor each morning to the time we close our eyes at night, who do we see, or hear, or talk to?

Who do we observe in unusual or annoying circumstances? Could there be opportunities to live with purpose and to touch others for Christ in that unexpected trip to the doctor's office? What about the times we're stuck in the longest line *ever*. And it's not. Moving. The young mother in front of us, or the elderly man behind us is also stuck. Could we ask God to open our eyes and ears to those who need a kind word or listening heart?

In 1 Peter 3:15, the apostle gives us a heads-up about purpose and readiness. "But in your hearts revere Christ as Lord. Always be prepared to give an answer to everyone who asks you to give the reason for the hope that you have. But do this with gentleness and respect." If we are "prepared to give an answer," unplanned encounters in our days become holy moments—incredible opportunities to speak a word for our Lord.

While dining out, my pastor's family will ask their waitstaff for prayer needs before thanking God for the food. "We're going to thank God for our meal. Is there anything we can pray for you about?" Such a simple act. But what a powerful witness—to their children, and to the server. In an instant, this person knows they are *seen,* and they have intrinsic worth and value.

Asking God for spiritual sensitivity as we go about the ordinary, transforms our days into unique adventures. I've stopped to pay for a soft drink and the Lord has prompted me to speak for him. One cashier told me I looked, "all dressed up." I mentioned our church had a Christmas cantata that morning. She squinted and said, "What's a cantata?"

No one was in line behind me, so during the next minute or two, I got to share what our cantata—singing of the coming of Jesus—was all about.

I've walked in on women crying in public restrooms, strangers on the beach marveling at "mother nature," and medical technicians questioning the intricate design of the human body. I've stood in line at a mall to make Christmas purchases and overheard two soldiers talking in front of me. One said, "I don't need any more gifts. Man, I just need peace."

Inside, I've simply smiled. *Oh, Father, you're so fun. Yes, I will speak for you.* I can honestly say, that upon waking those particular mornings, I had no idea I would be called on to speak for Christ in a restroom, on the beach, during a doctor's appointment, or in the mall. But God knew. These were divine appointments. If I happened to be walking in a self-absorbed bubble—like I so often do—I would have missed huge doses of joy and the chance to join God in his work.

And in the interest of complete transparency, when God asked me to chime in on the beach that day, I balked. The girls were playing, and I was toes-in-the-sand deep in me-time and a good book. When the woman approached me and attributed the beauty of the day to mother nature, I knew the Lord wanted me to speak for him. In stubborn obstinance, I resisted—until my ten-year-old daughter looked at me in expectation. She was, um, *waiting* for her mom to step up and speak up.

The moment I did, peace flooded me, and God was glorified. Just a simple, "Yes, it *is* a glorious day. Our Creator God is so amazing and artistic!" Admiring the day's glory opened the door to making a human connection in the Lord's name.

The instant we decide to live for Jesus, we receive a straight-from-heaven infusion of purpose and direction. We can never doubt where our field of service and influence might be—we are *living it* each and every day.

We've received our orders and there's no age exclusion. Can we trust that God is in control of our past, present, and future? Can we be faithful where he has placed us?

Oh, Lord, open my eyes to your work all around me. May my heart be sensitive to opportunities to be your precious hands and feet in my unique corner of this world. And thank you, Father, for calling me to a life of depth and passion.

In the Zone

Make a note of those you encounter in a typical week. Pray for wisdom to see each one as image-bearers of our Creator God. Look for open doors to share Christ through a kind word of encouragement.

Echoes of Faith

Charm is deceptive, and beauty is fleeting; but a woman who fears the LORD is to be praised. (Proverbs 31:30)

To this enterprising wife, mother, and businesswoman, middle-aged angst was a waste of time and emotion. Who cared? She had living to do. She and her husband worked and sacrificed to build a thriving business around fabric, sewing, and watch repair. Her skills as a seamstress were sought after and admired, and her Singer sewing machine enjoyed a steady whir of success.

As the business grew and became an establishment in the community, she raised three children—a boy and two girls. Active in her church, she taught her children to worship and serve God. She loved the Lord, her husband, and her family with a fierceness that left no doubt as to her loyalties. Life was busy, full, and meant to be tackled.

In her mid-forties, she became a grandmother and was so thrilled to meet her first granddaughter, she wore two different shoes to the hospital. What could be more important than holding this new little life?

To my knowledge, this woman—my grandmother—didn't squander a single minute longing for the past. Life was *now.* And it was rich and fun—an adventure of epic proportions.

My memories of my sweet granny include countless road trips, sleepovers, and breakfasts of pancakes fried until they were perfectly crisp around the edges. She could make the world's best pound cake (as long as she didn't slip in a touch of lemon), and her banana sandwiches were as much fun to watch her construct as they were to eat.

Granny was a professional dieter (her only nod to the changes of middle age). Every time we saw her, she would proudly announce how much weight she'd lost since the previous visit. Over the years, the tally had to be in the hundreds of pounds, but to me, she always looked the same—fit, fun, and forever my playmate.

But my sweetest memories center around holding Granny's hand and walking to Sunday school ahead of my parents—me in a puffy dress and tiny patent leather shoes, and her in a modest, handmade dress with sensible flats. She would talk and point and *listen* to my childish musings. And oh, how she would laugh—deep and rich and at nothing in particular.

This woman exuded joy.

When I think of my granny, my thoughts shift to a grandmother who received a loving mention in 2 Timothy 1:5. "I am reminded of your sincere faith, which first lived in your grandmother Lois and in your mother Eunice and, I am persuaded, now lives in you also." The apostle Paul is writing to the young Timothy to encourage him in the faith. Paul reminds Timothy that the seeds of his faith were planted at a young age—through his mother and grandmother.

Timothy's grandmother, Lois, had no way of knowing her simple acts of speaking and teaching of God would reach through the generations and touch so many. Did this saint of old pull little Timothy into the warmth of her lap and share stories of God's faithfulness? Did she set an example of loving Jesus by loving her neighbors? Did she place into practice the words of Moses in the ancient Scriptures?

"These commandments that I give you today are to be on your hearts. Impress them on your children. Talk about them when you sit at home and when you walk along the road, when you lie down and when you get up. Tie them as symbols on your hands and bind them on your foreheads. Write them on the doorframes of your houses and on your gates" (Deuteronomy 6:6–9).

Hundreds of years later, we honor the memory of Lois and stand amazed at the echoes of her influence.

Like Lois, my grandmother loved Jesus. Her son, my dad, grew into manhood, married, and with my mom, taught their children the ways of God. My husband and I had the privilege of teaching our children to love Jesus. And now, our call, our *mandate* is unchanged. We are to share with our children's children, and with anyone else the Lord places in our paths.

When we rest in the eternal perspective of God's plan of redemption reaching through the generations, mid-life dread becomes a non-issue.

These years are flooded with fresh opportunities to speak words of life, love, and joy.

To live in such a way, that our legacy of faith echoes throughout eternity.

Dear Father, thank you for the godly influence of those who have gone before me—who have walked with you and have shown me your ways. I pray for wisdom, Lord, and for a growing faith, that I may continue their legacy.

In the Zone

Make a list of treasured examples in the faith, including family, teachers, and friends. Praise God for their influence and ask him for an awareness of those who may long for Christ-centered leadership from you.

Give Me Less!

But I have calmed and quieted myself, I am like a weaned child with its mother; like a weaned child I am content. (Psalm 131:2)

Since speeding through my forties and now my fifties, one of the biggest adjustments has been my response to jarring noise. My tolerance for a restaurant's music and conversation buzz has diminished along with my ability to absorb input from multiple sources at once. If my sweetheart has the television competing with the radio, while he strums on his twelve-string, I fantasize about joining a monastery and making vows of silence and seclusion.

My brain wants to explode, but instead, begins to shut down. Am I the same woman who could corral dozens of children at a time into various activities? The same mom who could simultaneously listen to the radio, answer a child's question, and plan the family menu for the coming week? What happened?

In addition to the natural physical changes of age, could this also be the way our Lord calls us into his presence? Because the older I become, and the closer I grow to him, the more I long to still and quiet my soul.

The more I long for *less*.

Oh, how I want less worry, and a stronger dependence on the one who created me. Less busyness, and more focus on people and activities that provide fulfillment in Christ. Less timidity, and increased boldness to live with victory and purpose. Less noise, and an inner life of stillness and peace.

Less stuff, and more *life*.

But for this to happen, I must experience a wave of discontentment. I must be utterly dissatisfied with a life on cruise control—floating through each day without thought. I must be oh-so-sick with hours of mindless television, empty activity, and squandered days.

My cellphone has an application that breaks down our time together—including social media—for me and my little phone-buddy. The first time I saw the statistics for the week, I was mortified. *Surely not! There's no way I was on my phone that much.* The stats didn't lie. That little rectangular box had an unwelcome hold on my life and priorities.

Enough!

How Romans 8:6 touches a place deep within us. "The mind governed by the flesh is death, but the mind governed by the Spirit is life and peace." We long for our lifeblood to flow with substance and vitality.

The world encourages us to worship the status quo—to bow to the gods of cultural trends and to drown in an existence of go, go, *go*. God calls us to lives of freedom, adventure, and *abundance*. To engage and build relationships with depth and texture. To leave our corners of the world a little sweeter and brighter, and with a longing for things of heaven. But how can we do this if we're spending ridiculous amounts of time with our gadgets and our stuff?

Psalm 37:4 reads, "Take delight in the LORD, and he will give you the desires of your heart." There's a fascinating component to this verse. When we delight in our Lord, he moves in us to grow us into his image. Our thought-life is changed. Our wants and needs are transformed. We become more in tune with the Holy Spirit and our spirits agree with the mind of Christ.

Nurturing that stillness deep within us is vital if we are going to make a difference where we are. Matthew 5:13–16 reads: "You are the salt of the earth. But if the salt loses its saltiness, how can it be made salty again? It is no longer good for anything, except to be thrown out and trampled underfoot. You are the light of the world. A town built on a hill cannot be hidden. Neither do people light a lamp and put it under a bowl. Instead they put it on its stand, and it gives light to everyone in the house. In the same way, let your light shine before others, that they may see your good deeds and glorify your Father in heaven."

Our peers look and long for something of substance and value, and the peace, light, and life-flavor they witness within us can be the spark God uses to draw them to himself.

What a unique opportunity to extend God's grace and peace, and what an incredible responsibility. As we seek to reach others through divine stillness and light, we show others what an amazing Savior we serve!

Precious Father, I don't want to exude the smelly fumes of a frantic life. I want to carry the fragrance of you—your peace and your stillness. Oh, Father, I long for less of this world and more of you!

In the Zone

Seek stillness and rest in God's presence as you meditate on these verses: Psalm 5:3, Psalm 130:5, and Psalm 62:5. Keep a copy of one or more of these Scriptures handy as you go about your day.

Forever Mom

Do not be anxious about anything, but in every situation, by prayer and petition, with thanksgiving, present your requests to God. (Philippians 4:6)

My cellphone buzzed to announce a new text message, and as I scrolled through the short missive, I had to smile. My youngest daughter was in the process of preparing a casserole for dinner, and she had a few questions. *So, I just mix it all together? And it cooks for how long?*

If you have adult children, you know exactly what I was feeling in the moment—a sense of joy and thankfulness. Because even though it was a few simple inquiries about a recipe, my little girl needed me. She picked up the phone and texted *me*, her mom. And in this culture of Google searches and YouTube instructional videos, this was a pretty big deal.

In this season of endless transition, our relationships with adult children continue to evolve. The experience can seem quite surreal. We move from full-time hands-on parenting to if-you-need-me-I'm-here momhood—all in the course of the fastest eighteen years of our lives.

As my friend, Jeannie, prepared to let go of her college-aged daughter, her mind flooded with concerns. "I gave birth, nurtured, raised, nursed, cheered, taught, and encouraged for years! How will she know what to do? Will she remember all I've taught her? Maybe I should tell her ..."

When this mom returned from helping her daughter settle at school, the Holy Spirit began a work in her heart. "I longed to talk and to hug again as soon as we'd left her. But I refrained from calling frequently. The joy was in the fact that she called me daily, then every other day, then every few days until she'd established herself into a college routine. We still talk often now that she's married and has a baby. I think giving her some space sweetened our relationship."

Jeannie worked to give her children room to grow—without the unsolicited advice from a hovering parent. She respected their adulthood and slipped into the supportive role of champion and if-needed advisor. Through the guidance of the Holy Spirit, she strengthened the foundation of a rich and beautiful friendship with her children.

But what if our children don't ask for our opinions and insights? From our perspective, what if they need to reevaluate certain actions or decisions? How do we provide love and affirmation while honoring new boundaries?

In *Blessing Your Grown Children* by Debra Evans, she writes—"Parents bless their grown children when they accept the fact that their children are now responsible for their own decisions. Parents can no longer prescribe the course of their children's lives nor manage the events and experiences that come their way."

The author continues with great insight: "To truly bless our children, we respect not only their independence, but we also let them manage the consequences that come from their choices. Of course, our prayers can always beg God for the best for them, but our response to them should not be one of picking up the pieces all the time. They get the joys and problems that come from their choices."[7]

Our prayers can always beg God for the best for them.

This is the key. This is the honor and privilege of touching our children's lives with the power and influence of heaven. Prayer is never a last resort—a this-is-all-I-can-really-do answer to our worries. Approaching the throne of grace on behalf of our children is *the* answer—the most powerful, effective action to be taken.

As we pray God's word over the ones we love, we are infused with strength and hope, and we can rest in the knowledge that he loves our children with an enduring faithfulness.

What does it look like to pray God's word? Consider the following examples.

Lord, I want my son (or daughter) to have a sense of awe when thinking of you—that he will be flooded with fear and respect, and his heart will tremble in your presence (based on Proverbs 9:10).

Oh, Father, may my child have an attitude of submission. I pray she will cease fighting and rationalizing her will. May her soul be flooded with love, thankfulness, and overwhelming humility—*and may her heart be one with yours* (based on James 4:10).

Father, I pray that my child will seek you with all her heart and will not lean on her own understanding. I pray she will look to you in her decision making and will trust you to direct her paths (based on Proverbs 3:5–6). *And Lord, may she be strong and courageous and remember that you are with her in every step she takes* (based on Joshua 1:9).

There's no secret formula for effective praying. James 5:16 reads: "The prayer of a righteous person is powerful and effective." Honestly, this verse used to make me uncomfortable. I would lament, *but Lord, I'm not righteous!*

God showed this clueless girl I'm not petitioning the throne of heaven in *my* righteousness, but in *his*. In the deepest places of my heart, every prayer begins with, *Father God, I pray in, under, and through the righteousness of Jesus.*

What a relief to claim his authority and not our own!

Oh, the joy of petitioning our Lord to cover our children with a spirit of purpose, compassion, maturity, holiness, trust, submission, reverence, and more.

Oh, the power of a praying mom!

Father God, in my ever-changing role as mom, may I be a steady source of support and encouragement. I seek your wisdom and guidance that I may be a Christ-centered influence—one who will seek to build with affirmation and not destroy with criticism. Lead me, Father. And thank you for this precious gift of motherhood.

In the Zone

Read Ephesians 1:17–19, Philippians 4:19, and Proverbs 4:23. Use these Scriptures as prayer-starters over your children or grandchildren.

This Girl is on Fire

But those who hope in the LORD will renew their strength.
They will soar on wings like eagles; they will run and not
grow weary, they will walk and not be faint. (Isaiah 40:31)

As my friend Charla and I met over McDonald's finest cuisine and
swapped stories of our midlife escapades, I'm sure the clusters of teenagers
dining nearby wondered about the *mature women* giggling in the corner.
They may have thought we were performing strange, ancient dance moves
as we waved our arms over our heads and propped a fist on one hip before
erupting in unbridled laughter.

The moves were really quite simple. We were sharing ways to use a hair
dryer without showcasing our middle-aged "bat-wings." You know, just in
case our better halves were close by and watching. Because, seriously, even
after all these years, I'm not crazy about my husband seeing my "abundance"
dangling beneath my upper arms.

And the fist on the hip? The proper way to pose for pictures, of course.
That's how the younger crowd does it. Bring out a camera or cellphone,
and their adorable skinny selves turn sideways and place a hand on the hip
quicker than you can say *selfie*. Another tip? Squeeze or clinch the biceps
while posing—a guaranteed way to diminish the wings.

We also decided to relax with our exercise routines. We receive regular
workouts each night from flinging the bedcovers across the room. Surely
all that extra heat burns calories.

And for quick heat relief, lean inside the refrigerator or freezer, stand
outside (coat-less) in sub-freezing weather, or simply close all window
coverings and showcase your best undies. With the price we pay for them,
it's a shame they're hidden from view, anyway.

How in the world can our bodies morph into something we don't even recognize? Wasn't puberty and childbirth enough? What are we to make of hot flashes, night sweats, gray hair, and weight gain? And when did it become a major endeavor to sit on the floor without wondering how we'll get back up? I mean, seriously. How are we to live as vibrant, passionate women when we feel so *icky*?

There's an answer of supernatural proportions. God has gifted his children with a precious secret more fascinating than the greatest magic. This remedy appears illogical, but it radiates with truth.

Ponder these words from 2 Corinthians 4:16. "Therefore we do not lose heart. Though outwardly we are wasting away, yet inwardly we are being renewed day by day." If we had to define these years of fading strength and beauty, *wasting away* would be a perfect description. We long for more color, more elasticity, and more energy. But according to this verse, we're not to lose heart! Even as our outer selves change and show signs of wear, our inner selves—the heart and soul of us—is being renewed.

But how? Automatically? Just because God has compassion on us? Renewal happens as we walk with him and keep in step with his Spirit. As we tuck his word in our hearts. As we ponder his precepts and live in obedience.

Ready to feel a rush of youth? Check out Psalm 92:14: "They will still bear fruit in old age, they will stay fresh and green." Isn't this amazing? Fresh and green!

Ready for a smile? This verse is even richer in the King James Version of Scripture. "They shall still bring forth fruit in old age; they shall be fat and flourishing." Oh, how fun! We can be fat and flourishing for Jesus. Ah, a dream come true. Do I hear an *amen*?

And there's an extra perk of inner renewal. All that satisfaction and hope in Jesus will overflow and bubble to the surface. We *will* be on fire—and our countenance will shine with a peace that's hard to comprehend. Others will be drawn to Jesus in us. And doors will be opened to sharing the secret.

One super-hot flash at a time.

Oh, Father, sometimes I feel anything but fresh and green. I am often distracted by outer changes and I lose focus on what you desire to do in me.

As I seek your heart, I claim your promise of inner renewal and I praise you for the hope it brings. I long to be more like you!

In the Zone

In the last days and weeks, has your focus been on grieving outer physical changes? How does Isaiah 40:31 provide perspective?

A Fresh Touch

He refreshes my soul. He guides me along the right paths for
his name's sake. (Psalm 23:3)

Janice did her best to engage in small talk when we bumped into
each other in the frozen foods section of the grocery store. She asked the
appropriate questions and nodded in all the right places. But a second
look into her dark-rimmed eyes revealed an inner angst and bone-deep
exhaustion. In a season of caregiving for her parents, this weary woman
longed for a reprieve from constant worry and the never-ending physical
pace.

Tracy stood with a group of friends outside church and let their
upbeat chatter swirl around her. She had nothing to say. She felt as if she
was peering through a fog, unable to engage on any level—personal or
otherwise. Her workweek had stretched to fifty-plus hours and showed no
signs of abating. Her two high schoolers were in the middle of basketball
season, so it wasn't unusual to leave work after six and walk straight into a
gymnasium for several hours in the bleachers. Tracy longed to cherish her
children's remaining years at home, but she felt trapped under a mantle of
fatigue.

These precious women yearned for a time of renewal. For a few
moments to *breathe* and rekindle an inner strength and resolve. For the
fortitude to put one foot in front of the other.

We've all been there—a place where we are sure to drown in this thing
called life. Where the day-to-day seems a matter of survival and the idea of
abundant living seems like an unattainable religious catch-phrase.

This can be a dangerous place. Exhausted and overwhelmed, we are easy prey for the lies of darkness and unsound thinking. *I am so alone. No one could possibly understand what I'm feeling. Has God has abandoned me?* We gaze around us. Other women *seem* to exhibit better coping skills, so we tell ourselves to quit whining and keep moving—all while battling inner voices of disillusionment, disappointment, and sadness.

Where is God in this swirl of chaos?

In 1 Kings 19, the prophet Elijah found himself in crazy circumstances. He had experienced an emotional and spiritual high when the ground shifted beneath him and his world threatened to collapse. He was beyond tired. He was afraid for his life. His soul-shattered words in verse four sum it up: "I have had enough, Lord." After running from the threats of a crazy, vengeful Queen Jezebel, Elijah sat under a broom tree and prayed for death. *I have had enough, Lord.*

As we continue reading, we discover something extraordinary. God responds to the despair of his servant. "Then he [Elijah] lay down under the bush and fell asleep. All at once an angel touched him and said, 'Get up and eat.'" (v. 5) And again in verse seven: "The angel of the LORD came back a second time and touched him and said, 'Get up and eat, for the journey is too much for you.'"

Oh, how we respond to the suffering of Elijah! How often have our hearts cried out to God, *I have had enough. Please, Lord, I cannot take another step.* But do we recognize the hope in these verses? *Get up and eat, for the journey is too much for you.*

Pause. Breathe. Seek refreshment in the Living God.

The angel of the Lord touched Elijah. God listened and responded. God swept the lies from Elijah's weary mind. *I am here. You are not alone. I do care. This is a time of rest. Rest in me.*

Like Elijah, has the day-to-day been too much for us? Does it feel as if we've reached a breaking point? Are we tempted to crawl in a cave and hide under our favorite blanket with a bag of dark chocolate?

Sweets are always welcome, but more practical steps may include a deliberate change on the next pages of our day-planners. Do our schedules reflect Christ-centered priorities? Is it time to delegate, even temporarily, certain activities and responsibilities?

We must steamroll over the soul-shrinking lie that no one will understand our struggles. We can ask friends or family to sit with a loved one to provide an afternoon or evening to recoup. And the firmament will not collapse to the earth if we miss an occasional event with our children. Wouldn't our darlings prefer a mom not shuffling along in perpetual exhaustion?

There is help. There is hope. Our Lord is waiting with a heart of compassion. Let's speak to him from the depths of where we are and lean into his faithfulness.

Rest, dear one.

Please show me what to do, Lord. I need your wisdom. This weight of exhaustion grows so heavy and I long for a few moments of quiet peace and relief. Give me courage to ask for help and guide me to make needed changes in my schedule. Thank you, Father, for your faithful love.

In the Zone

Read 1 Kings 19 and take special note of how God spoke to Elijah. How can you allow time each day to listen for your Lord's gentle whispers?

The Perils of Solitary Confinement

Therefore encourage one another and build each other up,
just as in fact you are doing. (1 Thessalonians 5:11)

I remember the moment I felt the beginning rumbles of the midlife shift. In the car with my mom and my youngest daughter, we talked and chatted about anything and everything. At some point, my mom reached to find a radio station and settled back to enjoy the silky tones of Elvis Presley. In the back seat, my teenager engaged her iPod to listen to a popular boy-band. (I couldn't recall the name of said boy-band even under threat of bodily harm.)

Here I was—stuck in the middle. I wasn't drawn to either sound, so I sighed and half-listened to both. I had the strangest feeling that day of *where in the world do I belong?*

Young mothers have playdates and park meet-ups. In a group of peers, they immediately identify and enjoy a source of endless conversation. If one mother has a question, others will have multiple answers. They walk the same path and seek to support and nurture one another.

Seniors and retirees in our area meet for morning coffee and plan group travel. The local senior center is abuzz with endless activity—from exercise and craft classes to preparing for the senior Olympics. They are aware of group health needs and are eager to step up when needed.

And here we are—somewhere in this vast midlife zone. Most of us still clock in at work and some have older children at home or in college. We have slipped into a caregiving role with our parents or extended family. The months can slip by without meeting a friend for dinner or attending a missions or women's group. We place one foot in front of the other and do our best to *keep moving.*

The danger? The long shadow of isolation hovers and threatens. We become disengaged in our relationships and we succumb to Satan's lie that we are the *only ones* going through a specific trial or season of doubt. This master of evil loves to separate us from other believers, because he knows if we pull away from each other, we will wilt in endless solitude. We are easy prey for his lies.

But God's plan and design is rich, full, and the exact opposite of this! Our Creator calls us *to stop listening to the lies.* Psalm 16:11 reads, "You make known to me the path of life; you will fill me with joy in your presence, with eternal pleasures at your right hand."

There is no disclaimer with this verse. The words aren't contingent on our seasons of life or the pile of stuff on our plates. Yes, life is busy. Yes, we are in a different place.

But God is where we are. He is with us in each moment, each *breath.* When we come to him and seek his heart, he will *make known* the path of our lives. He will fill us with *joy* in his presence!

And what joy and wonder is available as we journey with each other. "As iron sharpens iron, so one person sharpens another" (Proverbs 27:17). We need each other! We may not all be wired to be best friends, but we can love, respect, and grow together as fellow image-bearers of the Most High God.

With the power of God working in us, let's avoid the trap of moving through life with a self-focused mindset. As we pray through our inner fog, we will look to our right and our left, thrilled to see fellow travelers. And these faces will be just as excited to see us there.

We are never alone in this season. With one hand, hold on to the Lord—the source of all life and abundance. With the other hand, link fingers with the sister beside you.

May we take joy in each other!

Dear Lord, thank you for sisters in the faith and for the joys of traveling in step with each other. May I remember that Christ-honoring companionship is from you. May I glorify you in my friendships.

In the Zone

Examine your circle of influence, including work, church, and community. Who are those who need a tender smile and a word of encouragement? Pray for open doors to explore deeper friendships.

Creative Prayer

Pray continually. (1 Thessalonians 5:17)

Shelley's daughter approached her in exasperation. "Mother, how are you praying?" Fighting a smile, this mother's heart leaped with hope and amusement because she knew the source of her child's frustration.

When her children made unhealthy dating choices, this creative mom didn't fret. She simply got busy. She petitioned the Lord for specific things in a date, including an unpleasant body odor or an irritating laugh. And now, Shelley consistently prayed for her daughter's boyfriend—that he would seem, um, *undesirable*. She prayed for unexplainable irritations between them and a tendency to get on each other's nerves.

The Holy Spirit guided this mom to breathe prayers she would never think of on her own. Body odor? An odd laugh? As she committed her children to the Lord, she saw answers to her petitions. Her daughter felt indeed irritated by her new friend and the relationship soon ended.

This creative prayer warrior also made a commitment. She and her husband held firm on house rules—regardless of how violently a child pushed. She leaned on Joshua 1:9 which reads, "Have I not commanded you? Be strong and courageous. Do not be afraid; do not be discouraged, for the LORD your God will be with you wherever you go."

Many times, her prayers went beyond a request for simple irritations. In seasons of sorrow, when children turned their backs on God's ways, Shelley spent hours on her face before the throne of heaven—begging God to intervene and seeking his heart and will on behalf of her precious ones.

As one child became trapped in substance abuse, she clung to Psalm 119. Verses 30–31 became the prayer of her heart. "I have chosen the way of faithfulness; I have set my heart on your laws. I hold fast to your statutes, LORD; do not let me be put to shame."

Charla sat across from her college-age son over lunch and felt a check in her spirit. God's whisper was firm and distinct: *That's enough.*

The spirit-filled words brought a mixture of relief and uncertainty. This devastated mom gazed on her son and attempted to reconcile the boy she nurtured into manhood with the young man who calmly declared his intentions to live a lifestyle contrary to God's plan and design. Charla knew hearts would be broken—hers, her husband's, and the very heart of God.

With a strength not her own, she reminded her son of the truth of God's Word. From her very core, she shared sorrows *and hopes* for his repentance and renewal.

But now, a divine stop sign. An internal conviction to wait. And to trust.

In an attitude of surrender, Charla lay her burdens at the feet of Jesus. She made a commitment to follow the Spirit's leading in her conversations with her son. She and her husband pledged to keep their home open to him—their hearts and ears ready when needed. Charla's voice continues to ring with intensity. "Legalism broke me a long time ago. If we close our door, where will he hear the truth?"

And they pray. With a creative intensity, they fall at the foot of the cross, beseeching God for their son's brokenness and for his deliverance from the darkness of Satan's lies. They continue to love—to gift their son with unconditional devotion and patience.

In spite of the insanity swirling around their families, Shelley and Charla vowed to remain true to God's precepts. As a result, their faith continues to grow and strengthen. In unimaginable circumstances, they seek to glorify God and to live as loving anchors for their families.

Shelley and Charla would be the first to tell us their prayers are rarely pretty. They can be messy and disjointed. But the Holy Spirit moves, and works, and intercedes. He empowers these lion-hearted women to put on the full armor of God and to fight for their children.

What about us? Do we need to ask God to guide us in creative prayer? Maybe it's time to pray that the world's glitter will taste like cardboard in our children's mouths. That shallow living will make them nauseous with distaste and dissatisfaction. That they would be driven to their knees, their wills broken, their hearts longing for restoration.

Is it odd to want our children to be uncomfortable? To request divine action—no matter the cost—on their behalf? Is this kind of praying *dangerous*?

Or is it infinitely more reckless to watch our children teeter on the edge of eternity and neglect the most powerful recourse available?

Philippians 2:13 gives the needed perspective. "For it is God who works in you to will and to act in order to fulfill his good purpose." As we seek God's heart and mind, the Holy Spirit guides our thoughts and petitions. *For it is God who works in you.*

Our hearts will skip a beat as we recognize words and prayers flowing from our lips that originated in the heart of Christ. Our confidence will take wing as we enter the Most Holy Place in the righteousness of our Savior.

In Jesus, our prayers over our children are powerful and effective. And each appeal, each *plea*, will enrich our worship and refine us into the women we were created to be.

One creative prayer at a time.

Precious Father, my deepest longing is to continue in an attitude of prayer over my children. Please guide my petitions according to your perfect will. Thank you, Jesus.

In the Zone

Meditate on Psalm 42:8, 1 John 5:14, and Psalm 19:14. Trust God to guide your soul-deep petitions for your loved ones.

The Makings of a Good Sandwich

> Praise be to the God and Father of our Lord Jesus Christ, the Father of compassion and the God of all comfort, who comforts us in all our troubles, so that we can comfort those in any trouble with the comfort we ourselves receive from God. (2 Corinthians 1:3–4)

Jan swiped at rogue tears and did her best to focus on the surrounding traffic during her two-hour drive home. At the moment, life seemed ... barren. Which was worse? Driving *away* from her baby-girl college student or driving *toward home* where her husband recently lost his job, and her father was losing a heart-wrenching battle with Alzheimer's disease?

For months, each day had been a chaotic swirl of impossible decisions—her roles of wife and daughter morphing into a season of role-reversals as her husband and parents looked to her for mental and emotional support. Under intense pressure, there were moments when Jan wondered if she would be able to stand under the weight.

In the center of the storm, when her knees threatened to buckle, this troubled woman chose to kneel. "I prayed so much. So hard."

Jan was gifted with the ability to plan and organize, but under extreme duress, she knew she needed help. A caregiving class gave her priceless insights into her parents' lives, and over time, God opened her eyes to needs outside of her immediate focus. Ministry opportunities abounded as she reached out to others walking the same journey—giving and receiving strength.

Michelle moved through her mother's home and changed lightbulbs, stocked the pantry, and deep-cleaned each room. She worked methodically, mentally checking each task as completed. Throughout the busy days, she was *with* her mother, but her *thoughts* were three states away with her son in college.

As she completed the required duties and gathered her things to begin the grueling trip home, her heart was convicted of a gaping hole of neglect. Lost in the practical aspects of the visit, this exhausted caregiver had forgotten to seek moments of stillness with her beloved mother or to initiate sustained eye contact.

Michelle's heart squeezed in a time of quiet reflection. *In these hours of care, did I have a genuine connection with Mom?* As feelings of failure threatened to break her heart, the Holy Spirit flooded her fragile thoughts with hope. "For I am the Lord your God who takes hold of your right hand and says to you, Do not fear; I will help you" (Isaiah 41:13).

Her spirit quickened with joy and relief. With fresh resolve, Michelle asked the Lord to sharpen her vision and for the strength to discern her mother's spiritual needs as well as the physical. In future visits, she slowed her pace and cherished the simplicity of sitting next to her mother, watching her eyes and expressions. She took joy in the silences and moments of gentle laughter.

Laden with additional responsibilities, Jan and Michelle were not simply part of a generational sandwich, but more like a triple-decker *club* sandwich. Hard-pressed on all sides, they found themselves navigating the needs of multiple generations and facing unique pressures and events.

Have you been there? You're suddenly asked to make life-altering decisions for someone who has always guided *your* way. A parent reaches out on the home phone at the same time your high schooler calls your cell phone. Pulled and stretched, you long to honor and respect your parents' needs—to be sensitive and available—but you're still in the hands-on parenting years.

These are soul-searching times and honest questions are needed. If God has allowed our present circumstances, will he provide the resources needed to thrive in this season? Through the difficult days, will we allow God to complete his work in us, to make us more like him? Could our service be *worship?* "Therefore, I urge you, brothers and sisters, in view of God's mercy, to offer your bodies as a living sacrifice, holy and pleasing to God—this is your true and proper worship" (Romans 12:1).

The time is now to redefine the whole "sandwich" concept. Instead of succumbing to the cultural expectations of caught-in-the-middle misery, what if we saw ourselves as part of a *divinely blessed hero* sub? At our foundation, God's faithfulness and eternal presence. Ahead, God's provision, guidance, and promise.

And in the middle? You and me—nestled in the midst of steadfast hope and strength—abiding in Christ with each challenge. Trusting him with our sorrows and disappointments. Seeking open doors to extend compassion on the journey.

Each circumstance—each hurdle—topped and covered with time in the Word and wrapped in the everlasting arms.

Now *that's* the makings of a good sandwich.

Abba, Father, through the difficult days, may I look to you for strength and perspective. May the works of my hands be pleasing to you and may serving others become a beautiful way to bow in worship. Yes, Jesus.

In the Zone

Read 2 Corinthians 4:8–10. If you are struggling with feeling "hard pressed," ask God to give you a fresh perspective and a renewed heart for service. Ask a trusted friend to pray for your specific needs. Take comfort in knowing that shared burdens grow lighter.

Stylin' and Profilin'

But let your adorning be the hidden person of the heart with
the imperishable beauty of a gentle and quiet spirit, which
in God's sight is very precious. (1 Peter 3:4 ESV)

Shelley completed a slow twirl in front of her bedroom mirror. Eyeing
the new outfit—black tights and short plaid skirt—her heart skipped,
and she gave the skirt a downward tug. *Too short?* A recent weight loss led
Shelley to purchase new clothing, and the euphoria of wearing a smaller
size and a younger, trendier style worked its way through her body and
lit her face with a victorious smile. Ignoring the check in her spirit, she
grabbed her purse and headed to work.

Her victory grin increased in size—until she arrived at the office. The
church office. Where she served as children's ministry leader alongside her
pastor-husband.

Shelley's goal had been to surprise her sweetheart—to make his eyes,
"pop out of his head." But to her dismay and supreme embarrassment, the
entire church staff barely controlled *their* eye-popping reactions, and she
slipped home, mortified, to change clothes. "I felt like I was pretending to
be a young school girl. I kicked myself on the way home. *Oh, man, you are
so dumb.*"

Later that afternoon, the mistake didn't sting as much when her
husband gave her a wink and a smile and said she didn't need to return the
skirt.

I can relate to Shelley's red-faced experience. I've shopped and admired
various styles, only to have a young clerk quietly direct me out of the *junior*
department. I've drooled over cute tops with leggings, tight jeans with
"awesome" holes in the knees, and off-the-shoulder sweaters. I've ordered

the coolest outfits online, only to model the clothes at home, give a groan, and tuck the teen-leaning garments in the back of a drawer. *Never* to be seen again (um, outside our home).

I've wondered, *why is this so hard?* I want to be current, stylish, comfortable, and appropriate. I want to appear polished and together without dressing like a fifteen-year-old or someone 102. Is this too much to ask?

If you're like me, this middle season has given me a love for all styles tunic-y. Don't you simply *love* the tunic? Pretty, flowy, with the ability to camouflage most anything. Inside tip: Cracker Barrel Old Country Store carries myriad choices in the tunic family. They also offer biscuits. A connection? Hmm.

Honestly, I would wear T-shirts and jeans every day of my life. I'm extremely grateful the television program *What Not to Wear* went off the air. My blood pressure spiked each time I realized I didn't measure up to their perfect, adorable, completer-piece, cardigan-draped standards. If the beautiful hosts explained how to buy jeans *one more time*, I would've sent a pillow-missile across the room. Or turned the channel, whichever sped up the process.

I'll admit, most of my style issues are caused by concerns over what others will think. *Look at her, she's trying to be a teenager.* Or, *bless her heart, that dress makes her look twenty years older.* I've never actually heard someone utter these judgments, but they've reverberated through my paranoid brain, nonetheless.

In my own home, I'll admit to savoring holey jeans and soft leggings, but in public, I never want my clothing to be a distraction, or cause someone to question my motives. I want the focus to be on honoring the one who created me. How can I effectively share Jesus if someone is preoccupied with the way I dress?

As Christian women, our goals for how we present ourselves to the world have substance and purpose. Proverbs 31:25 begins with, "She is clothed with strength and dignity." 1 Corinthians 6:19–20 reads, "Do you not know that your bodies are temples of the Holy Spirit, who is in you, whom you have received from God? You are not your own; you were bought at a price. Therefore honor God with your bodies." And Isaiah 61:3 speaks of being clothed with praise instead of despair.

We can honor our Lord without settling for being a bland colorless mess. We can learn what colors complement our complexions. We can wear styles that flatter our shapes. And we can place an emphasis on never leaving home without our completer-piece.

The beautiful, ever-popular, *always-in-style*, garment of praise.

Lord, I never want my outward appearance to be a distraction from bringing glory to you. Convict my heart to be clothed in your love, compassion, and praise so that all focus remains on you.

In the Zone

With 1 Corinthians 6:19–20 in mind, conduct an honest appraisal of your dressing habits. Is there anything that deflects honor from the Lord?

The Birds and the Bees and Aching Knees

My beloved is mine and I am his. (Song of Solomon 2:16a)

Once upon a time, a starry-eyed young couple sat on a hill amidst glorious spring blooms and shared heart-dreams for the future. They spoke of life and love, how many pitter-patters of feet would fill their home, and what they would name each one. The breeze swirled around them and the sun shone with hope and promise.

The boy sat mesmerized by her loveliness and sense of adventure. *Lord, what did I do to deserve her?*

The girl hung on his every word. *My husband is the most handsome, bravest, smartest man in the entire world.*

And they smiled. A lot. Simply sitting with fingers entwined was enough. With God, they could conquer any challenge. Face any obstacle. And love fiercely through it all.

Fast-forward thirty-five years. Our pitter-patters—all three sets of them—pattered their way into lives of their own. Memories wash over us, as we relive the blur of parenting babies, to toddlers, to teens, to young adults. We catch our breath at the waves of endless spiritual warfare and the years of letting go.

The house is quiet. Dreams have been realized, reshaped, forgotten, and abandoned.

Hands are still entwined, but their appearance has changed. Tiny lines adorn each one, each a story on the journey. Blue eyes are fading. Once dark hair is now mostly gray.

And oh, the adventures. Years flooded with the makings of a life—the incredible mix of heartache and joy, sorrow and celebration, disappointment and achievement, disillusionment and triumph, anger and contentment.

A little stunned to be ushered into this season so quickly, we wonder about the next steps. Is there still time to dream? Can marriage still be *fun*?

In the crazy pace of raising a family, we may be out of practice with this couple stuff. We might not have the same reserves of strength and energy, but marriage can still be an adventure. God has a plan for these years!

When the girls were little, our designated date nights were sacred. We cherished our time to reconnect and focus on each other, without the demands of parenting. Those precious evenings and weekends away strengthened our love and friendship and renewed our commitment to our family and each other.

I assumed that a quiet house would lead to increased quality time with my sweetheart, but I've discovered that romance still requires an intentional investment. Oh, how easy to fall asleep on the couch in front of the television or stay engrossed in social media and other mindless pursuits. And what happened to our creativity? Somewhere along the road of enchantment, date nights morphed into dinner out and cruising through the local home improvement store or Walmart. Or both.

Our restless hearts rebel. *Where's the excitement?*

Ponder this Scripture from Song of Solomon 8:6–7: "Place me like a seal over your heart, like a seal on your arm; for love is as strong as death, its jealousy unyielding as the grave. It burns like blazing fire, like a mighty flame. Many waters cannot quench love; rivers cannot sweep it away. If one were to give all the wealth of one's house for love, it would be utterly scorned."

Wow. This is so *passionate*. But isn't this what we long for—a *blazing fire* and *a mighty flame*? Does this apply to mid-lifers married for decades? I was once challenged by a mentor to "keep the home fires burning." But what does this look like in this season?

Proverbs 3:3 is a love-challenge. "Let love and faithfulness never leave you; bind them around your neck, write them on the tablet of your heart."

Let love and faithfulness never leave you. We are called to remain loving and faithful—even when the hubby is annoying and leaves his clothes on the floor. When he needs a bigger belt and his hair is streaked with gray.

When he forgets important dates on the calendar or hasn't frequented the florist in ages.

But practicing love and faithfulness goes deeper than showing grace in the messiness of our days. It involves a commitment to explore. To mine the hidden gold in the men we married. To encourage them to be the warriors God created them to be—men of strength, dignity, and purpose.

The young girl who hung on the words of her beloved is now tempted to drift into her own thoughts and interests. I assume I've heard it all before. But have you noticed what happens when you give sincere focus, interest, and attention to the one you love? When you simply make *eye contact*?

He stands taller. His burdens are lighter. The assurance he's not alone strengthens each step.

The influence we have in our husband's lives cannot be understated. We can inspire, or we can cripple. We can show respect or disdain. We can pray for God's best or we can become a hindrance in their spiritual walk.

When's the last time we cheered them toward a new endeavor? Is there an ability or talent set aside in the years of shepherding a family? Is there an activity he's dreamed of trying? Is there something he wants us to explore together?

I have friends who have discovered unique ways to love their husbands. They've learned to fish, watched football without complaining, or climbed on the back of a motorcycle. Debbie made her husband a happy camper—literally. Weekends are filled with traveling and exploring the great outdoors.

Rene honors her spouse by resisting the lure of busyness—even with good things like church and extended family activities. She's discovered that being overscheduled robs them of precious couple time.

My friend Christine strapped on a parachute and jumped out of a plane! A smile lights her face as she gushes about the thrill she will *never* do again. But what a shared memory!

My sweetheart and I recently traveled out West and included a day at Hoover Dam. Wanting this to be a memorable trip, I promised myself I wouldn't rush through the exhibits and the tour of the dam. This was *his* thing and I knew he would read every word of every plaque. I found a seat and encouraged my love to linger and enjoy.

Two hours later, he emerged from the exhibit hall grinning like a teenager with his first car. He was excited and fulfilled, and his grin took me back to the man I married. Our hands held a little tighter the remainder of the day.

There's a mysterious magic woven throughout a covenant marriage—one built on trust and respect. There's a depth to our passion and understanding that wasn't available in the early years. We thrill to watch each other soar. Our lives are enriched as we seek God's best in each other—as we nurture, pray, challenge, and cheer one another toward a life of abundance.

I wonder about the young couple on that solitary hill in a remote town of North Dakota. If they could have gazed into the future, would their plans have changed? Would their bold dreams have been tempered with fear and trembling? Would they have had the faith and fortitude to take the next steps?

I praise God for his gift of one day, *one moment* at a time. Because the moments teach us to trust. In the passage of time, we learn the maker of our days provides our journey's needs—the perfect daily portions of endurance and grace.

And the priceless, unfading, *unending* love of the Savior.

Dear Father, may I be a steadfast source of support and encouragement for my husband. May I extend kindness, grace, and compassion as we journey on this adventure you have given us. May my heart be drawn to prayer, instead of criticism, and love, instead of blame. Thank you, Father, for the gift of this precious man. May he continue to grow into a man after your heart. Thank you, Jesus.

In the Zone

Reread Song of Solomon 2:16. Praise God for your spouse and ask him to open your eyes to creative ways to extend love and respect. Pray about taking a bold step and trying something new for the one you love!

I Didn't Really Mean It

Because of the LORD's great love we are not consumed, for his compassions never fail. They are new every morning; great is your faithfulness. (Lamentations 3:22–23)

Connie gripped the phone as her stomach dropped and she fought a tidal wave of panic. Her youngest son, a United States Marine, had called to say he would be sent to Iraq.

We can surely sympathize with her initial heart-reaction of *no*. If met with the same news, my heart would rebel, and I would try to mom-fix the situation. But within seconds, an overriding sense of peace—an assurance of God's sovereignty—poured like precious oil over Connie's spirit, and the stunned mom was able to breathe.

Why? Because she was soul-prepared. She entrusted her children to the Lord years ago and now she could rest, fully confident in his plans. *God, wherever you send him.*

Connie is a beautiful example of committing her loved ones to God's care. In the same season, her three babies lived in places as far-flung as Alaska, Thailand, and Iraq. She and her husband built their home on a foundation of faith—dependence on the precepts and promises of God—regardless of circumstances. And now, the peace that surpasses all understanding gave them strength to live in joyful assurance.

What about us? We've prayed for our children for years—that God would bless and use them in his kingdom. We've longed for them to grow in strength and have a genuine heart for service. But what if this means we have to let go? What if God's plans for them involve living across the country? Or *out* of the country? Do we truly trust him with our children's lives and future?

My first impulse is to say, "Wait, Lord. All those prayers about my children serving you, I don't think you understood. I meant for them to *safely* serve you *close by their mother.*"

On any given day, I haven't a clue what my children are facing in the moment. One daughter and her husband are settling in another state—seeking to teach their children the mysterious ways of God and to influence their new community with the gospel. Our middle daughter is nurturing a family and is on the frontlines of the battle for life. Her work carries her into neighborhoods I could never imagine her going outside of God's purposes. And my baby girl has entered the glittering corporate world. My prayers plead for God to give her strength and wisdom in our Babylon-focused society.

My preferences would never include my girls living across the country or having careers that placed them at risk. My way would be considered safe, sweet, and normal. But oh, how my selfishness would rob them of lives of depth—lives of vibrancy and texture.

Do we honestly want our children to be sheltered from the life-strengthening aspects of the struggle? How can they walk in victory, if there is never a battle?

Corrie Ten Boom said, "There are no 'if's' in God's world. And no places that are safer than other places. The center of His will is our only safety—let us pray that we may always know it!"[8] This is beautiful, and it makes me feel good to say it. But do I believe it? Ms. Ten Boom was *not* saying there will be a quiet, bubble-wrapped life inside God's plans. This beautiful saint suffered unimaginable terrors at the hands of Hitler's madmen. But through it all, she abided in Christ. Imprisoned in a Nazi concentration camp, her sister Betsy's dying words are a testimony to us all: "There is no pit so deep that He is not deeper still."[9]

There will be hardship, and mental and physical distress. There will be suffering. And brokenness. In fact, our Lord was honest and direct with his group of wide-eyed disciples.

"Then Jesus said to his disciples, 'Whoever wants to be my disciple must deny themselves and take up their cross and follow me'" (Matthew 16:24). Our Savior's journey involved pain, and hurt, and unfathomable anguish. Because of his great love, he glorified the Father with every step.

But wait. We want our children to marry well, have beautiful, well-ordered homes, and gift us with many, many grandbabies. How does this reconcile with "take up their cross?"

I've heard the example given of our children as ready-to-sail ships in the harbor of our hearts and homes. We've invested a lifetime to build and launch these precious vessels. We smile with pride as they float in the safety of our influence. But what good is a mighty ship in the calm waters of the backyard pool? A ship was meant for the open seas!

If our heart's desire is for our children to *know God*—to have a soul-connection and to *walk with him in their moments,* the only option is to trust with open hands. To release them for God's purposes. To honor his will and calling on their lives.

If our time on earth is the only consideration, then letting go would be a ridiculous proposition. Absurd, even. But we know that these days are a training ground for eternity. Life—true, authentic life—is found only in the heart of the Creator.

As her oldest son prepared to leave for Thailand to serve as a missionary-teacher, Connie gazed on her child—this grown-up man of God—and spoke these words: "This is the great adventure."

What a priceless gift and what a precious benediction.

Yes, Lord. *Yes.*

Precious Father, I pray for courage to truly seek your heart and will for my children. May they walk in step with you and have a fearless reliance on your promises and precepts. Use them, Father. Stretch them. And may they grow in wisdom and be mighty warriors in your kingdom. Thank you, Jesus. I trust in your love and purposes.

In the Zone

Meditate on Jeremiah 17:7–8. Use this Scripture as a prayer-starter over your children.

You've Got a Friend in Me

One generation commends your works to another; they tell of your mighty acts. (Psalm 145:4)

To this day, I regret my careless words.

A young mother navigated her way through the church building—juggling her infant, purse, Bible, and diaper bag, while simultaneously keeping her toddler in sight. Her expression was not one of *here I am to worship*, but one of *here I am to survive*.

As we passed each other in the hallway, I could see her stress and fatigue. I don't remember my exact words, but I know they were insensitive and hollow—devoid of anything resembling encouragement. Something like, "You think it's tough now, wait until they're ..." You can fill in the blank. My message was clear—it will get worse. What you're experiencing doesn't compare to what's ahead. Toughen up and keep moving.

Oh, how I long to go back in time and wrap my arms around that sweet mom. To apologize and to offer genuine Spirit-led hope and support. To validate her life season with the reminder she's not alone. I would offer to *carry her stuff* or escort her toddler to Sunday school. I would be Jesus instead of inconsiderate me.

If we ask the Lord to open our spiritual eyes, this season is rich with opportunities in the ministry of mentoring. We've lived a few years and have the battle scars to prove it. How does God want to use our experiences—triumphs *and* failures—to help younger women? Are there practical ways to live out Titus 2:3–5? "Likewise, teach the older women to be reverent in the way they live, not to be slanderers or addicted to much wine, but to teach what is good. Then they can urge the younger women to love their husbands and children, to be self-controlled and pure, to be busy at home, to be kind, and to be subject to their husbands, so that no one will malign the word of God."

In this Google-any-answer culture, we may think mentoring is obsolete. But godly love and wisdom can be a lifeline for young women seeking to honor God in their careers, marriages, and homes. In a digital age, they long for the warmth of someone who has walked the same path and for hope-filled assurance on the way.

With three grown daughters, I want to be available, but I do my best to refrain from unsolicited advice. If an issue weighs on my heart and I feel the Holy Spirit's leadership, I will say, "Honey, I need to be Mom for a few minutes." The girls know my words are coming from love, not censure.

After talking with young women in their twenties and thirties, consistent themes were repeated and reminded me of what I longed for as a young wife and mother. Every woman mentioned *encouragement* in its various forms. An old-fashioned card in the mail. A text. A gift card for a cup of coffee. The simple act of coming alongside and meeting them on their terms and schedule (not calling at the kid's bedtimes or in the throes of getting out the door each morning).

Many expressed a need for acceptance and understanding instead of judgment, and for the freedom to say, "no" to activities "everyone else" was doing. They yearned for honesty, not platitudes. And to a woman, they *are aware* these years fly. But as they wrangle three babies under the age of six, *the moments crawl.*

As in other relationships, godly mentoring involves modeling grace. Walking in the Spirit is non-negotiable because we never know when God will nudge us toward a need. I recently received a text from a young woman I hadn't seen in years. She reached out from a chasm of sadness, and we spent the evening pouring over God's word and his heart for her. I praise God for the opportunity to minister in an area I had previously failed.

Mentorship involves tenderness and warmth, not our oh-so-natural tendencies toward apathy and indifference. Effective influence centers on God's timing and purposes—never on heavy-handed, unwelcome interference.

How do we become a mentor? By walking with God and seeking discernment and godly wisdom. By responding to the leadership of the Holy Spirit when he opens our eyes to women in need of kindness. By being prayerful, available, and approachable. And by trusting God with the assignments and *with the results.* We don't have to know all the answers, but if we're in communion with the spirit, we can be ready to offer guidance and a listening heart.

1 Thessalonians 5:11 is a call to action. "Therefore encourage one another and build each other up, just as in fact you are doing."

What a treasure and privilege to fall in step with younger women—to extend love, grace, and compassion on this incredible adventure called life. And to offer a priceless glimpse of Christ-centered purpose and perspective for the journey.

Dear Lord, I ask for a tender, sensitive heart and for the wisdom to recognize the needs of younger women. May I offer genuine encouragement over empty, powerless words. And may I always point to you as the ultimate source of joy and strength.

In the Zone

Make a list of the younger women in your circle of influence. Pray over each name and ask God for opportunities to be Jesus to them.

When Dreams Change

In their hearts humans plan their course, but the LORD establishes their steps. (Proverbs 16:9)

Her laughter brought smiles to the faces of those around her as she lovingly sparred with close friends in the church foyer. With a quick wit and easy smile, she navigated the crowd of Sunday worshippers, drawing strength from each conversation. As she moved to the exit, her steps slower than usual, her husband was never far from her side.

My friend, Mary, now in her fifties, is adjusting to an unexpected midlife. Years ago, she never dreamed she would one day face the loss of a beloved son. Where she once assumed this season would involve the exploration of empty nest perks, like the freedom to travel, she instead points her car toward her three-times-a-week dialysis appointments.

Mary shares her story with candor. "I wish for *normal,* something my life is not. I never dreamed my husband and children would be caring for me at this age. Or that I would lose a son. My husband and I were supposed to grow old together, you know, like *normal.*"

Across the church grounds, another friend moves with measured grace. Her smile speaks of an unusual depth of joy—found only through struggle and difficulty.

Daphine also works to harmonize past dreams with present realities. At the age of 49, a diagnosis of stage-one breast cancer threatened her orderly world. With methodical planning, chemotherapy, and the best doctors, she fought back against the disease and emerged a champion.

For seven years, Daphine leaned on her doctor's pronouncement of "cancer free." But in an illogical, most surreal moment, a different doctor informed her the cancer had returned—this time, with a vengeance. The magnitude of hearing the pronouncement of stage-four breast cancer sent a shockwave through her body—her life and faith rocked to the core. "I was so shocked, I almost laughed. I had *just been told* that I was still cancer free."

These women are on unimaginable journeys as they attempt to reconcile what-should-be with what-actually-is. Their faith has been pushed, stretched, and hammered with in-your-face reality. They've been catapulted from the comforts of the pew into the midst of battle—and have been forced to examine their foundations like never before. *What is real? What is true?*

What happens when this season—supposedly of new beginnings—ushers in the unwanted and the unexpected? When our perfect plans not only fray around the edges, but crumble as dust under the crush of job loss, financial ruin, illness, divorce, or loss of a loved one?

When the ground shifts beneath our feet, each hurdle or fearful circumstance looms as an impenetrable wall, and we are tempted to question what we've always thought to be true. *No, wait. God, where are you? How could you let this happen? Haven't I always served you? Lord, do you see me?* And as we stare in horror at the monstrous obstruction before us, we question the size and strength of our God. *Um, Lord, are you able to handle this one?*

Jeremiah 32:27 speaks to our doubts. "I am the LORD, the God of all mankind. Is anything too hard for me?" And Deuteronomy 31:6 reminds us we are not alone in battle. "Be strong and courageous. Do not be afraid or terrified because of them, for the LORD your God goes with you; he will never leave you nor forsake you."

As we cling to his word, God speaks and ministers to our spirits. He works in our prayers of anguish, as we lay our trampled hearts before him. He extends precious comfort in the arms of his people—through Christian family and friends. Our mighty God uses our circumstances to draw us to himself and to refine and renew us from the depths of our soul to the light in our eyes.

For Mary, each day is packed with adjustments as she learns to slow her pace and trust God with her future. Accustomed to the busyness of work and family care, she is learning to be still, physically and spiritually. She praises God for the gifts in her life—her family and trusted Christ-centered friends and counselors. This warrior is learning practical life-skills to face each hurdle. And she works to increase her spiritual toolkit, including a powerhouse of go-to verses tucked in her heart and mind.

God has gifted Mary with the ability to laugh in the midst of absurdity and to cherish the simple blessings she may have overlooked in the past. "I can still cook dinner for my husband and drive myself to dialysis. I love going out to dinner and taking joy in the 'normal.' I got to be a part of my granddaughter's baptism and to stand close by, take pictures, and share funny moments with my pastor."

On the anniversary of her son's death, Mary clings to 2 Corinthians 1:3–4. "Praise be to the God and Father of our Lord Jesus Christ, the Father of compassion and the God of all comfort, who comforts us in all our troubles, so that we can comfort those in any trouble with the comfort we ourselves receive from God."

Her words to us are a testimony. "Live each day that you're given. Be *thankful* for the day. Pray more. Focus on God. Hold on to times of worship."

After the second cancer diagnosis, Daphine realized her trust had been misplaced in the years of being cancer free. "I put my faith in doctors and science. I didn't think I needed to keep praying about it. Then I was overcome with questions and doubts. Did I work too much? Gain too much weight? Have too much stress? Why did the cancer come back?

"My first reaction to the devastating news was to begin planning my funeral. I couldn't see beyond that. Then I got back into the Word. As soon as my husband left for work each morning, I got my Bible. I was *hungry* for God's word. I went to the Psalms and read them over and over. I began to calm down and to accept my journey."

This woman of God has changed her thinking and her priorities. "I was materialistic, but no more. I treasure my friendships. I long for my children to be safe, happy, and settled in Christ."

Every four months, Daphine goes for a body scan to see if the cancer remains dormant or has reared its head in another location. "Laying on the scan table, I don't want to think of what the machine is finding in my body. I choose to focus on the twenty-third Psalm and other verses I've learned. I remind myself that the same power that raised Jesus from the dead is the same power inside of me."

Daphine searches for daily reminders of God's sovereignty—through Bible study, sermons, devotions, and encouragement from others. And as she shares her story, her voice reverberates with a quiet strength. "God will never leave or forsake me."

Mary and Daphine are beautiful models of trusting God—even in the chaos of this fallen world. In spite of stress, doubts, and uncertainties, they are learning to seek *life* in their moments, and to place their anxieties at the feet of Jesus.

They remind us of the joy and wisdom found in Psalm 51:10–12. "Create in me a pure heart, O God, and renew a steadfast spirit within me. Do not cast me from your presence or take your Holy Spirit from me. Restore to me the joy of your salvation and grant me a willing spirit, to sustain me."

Renewed. Restored. Refined. Oh, the depths of our Savior's love!

Father God, thank you for the testimonies of these treasured friends. I praise you for your work in their hearts and for the peace you provide. You are truly a never-ending source of hope, strength, and renewal. Thank you for the opportunity to use our struggles as a way to glorify your precious name.

In the Zone

With 2 Corinthians 1:3–4 in mind, think of how your trials and hardships can be used by God to comfort others. Praise God for his faithfulness in times of trouble and ask him to open the eyes of your heart to recognize opportunities for ministry.

With Boldness and Courage

See, I am doing a new thing! Now it springs up; do you not
perceive it? I am making a way in the wilderness and streams
in the wasteland. (Isaiah 43:19)

I love summer. To me, summer is flip-flops, shorts, T-shirts, and lazy
evenings on the front porch. Summer is an annual vacation from the
everyday-ness of life. June, July, and August mean a week or two to dig
my toes in the white sands of our favorite family beach and to tilt my face
toward sweet southern sunshine. In my starfish-studded mind, this season
rings with the laughter of little bodies dancing through the spray of a water
hose. Memories soar of picnics at the park and teaching little ones how to
wrangle an oversized ice cream cone. Time stands still in the hazy glow of
warmth, love, and life.

My heart sings a sentimental song about these months, because I know
they are short-lived. Letting go of summer means an end to late nights on
a squeaky porch swing and no more bare feet on a lush carpet of grass. The
days shorten. Time begins to move toward that old familiar life-speed.

In many ways, this transition into midlife has felt like saying goodbye
to summer. My family would testify about my reluctance to abandon the
beach and all things flip-flop-ish. If I could anchor myself to the sand, I
would!

As I write, a rainstorm pelts our windows, sending tiny glistening
rivulets over the glass. Early-autumn leaves cling to their waning source
of nourishment. As each intricately-designed leaf whirls a chaotic dance,
my heart identifies. *No, I don't want to let go. I want things to stay as they've
always been—fresh, green, and rich with hope and joy. Lord, I'm content with
the present and I don't see a need to move forward.*

But the Lord is teaching me that he didn't design us for one-seasonal living. He's given us *so much more*—a depth of days packed with exploration and growth. Days that are squandered in our futile attempts to grasp the wind-blown shifting sands.

I wonder if our Lord sighs at our forgetfulness. *Oh, child, don't you remember what's coming?*

As the leaves relinquish their tenuous hold, creation provides a dazzling path for our feet. We gaze in wonder at muted shades of yellow, orange, red, gold, and brown, and we marvel in delight at the transformation. Cooler air brings much-needed relief from the heat and a soft sweater and our favorite socks prepare us for the season of crisp mornings and cozy evenings.

The home where my husband and I raised a family nestles against a deep woodland, and in the summer and early fall, the dense foliage prevents me from seeing beyond the thick wall of trees at the edge. But as the towering timbers release their glory, another picture begins to emerge. Beyond the line of poplars, oaks, and pines, the forest floor slopes to a tiny creek, then rises in a steady upward climb. Even though we live in a fairly level area of North Carolina, the rolling wooded landscape provides the illusion of living in the foothills.

Each year, I am surprised and enchanted. I'm reminded of what I would miss if the trees never let go of their treasures.

This is a time to seek and explore. To pursue each allotted day with vision, purpose, and a heart of expectancy. To *stop clinging to the past* and to embrace the present with passion and hope—knowing that God continues his work in us.

And the next steps? The possibilities are as varied as the colors of autumn.

After navigating the never-ending details of her daughter's wedding, another friend named Mary launched her own business as a wedding consultant. This surprising endeavor came after a long, fulfilling career in education. She saw a need and walked through a shiny new door of potential.

April left the world of corporate accounting and delights in sharing her days with two granddaughters—seeing life anew through the eyes of toddlers. She traded dress pants and a desk for high chairs and sticky fingers.

In a place of fulfillment, April is ministering to her daughters' families and investing in the next generation.

Connie continues to influence her world through covenant prayer and through ministry in her church's library. In this small space lined with Christ-centered resources, she is an endless fountain of godly wisdom and mentoring—reaching children and adults with Scripture, encouragement, and a listening heart. Connie will be the first to tell us, "Our nest isn't empty. We're still there." Her God-given purpose didn't change when her children began their own journeys.

Jan seeks opportunities to help others love and care for family members with dementia or Alzheimer's disease. She wants to use her grueling personal journey to share knowledge, resources, and hope.

Many jump into new careers, run for local office, cherish the time to travel, enjoy grandchildren, or volunteer. The goal is not to be *busy*, but to glorify God with our gifts, abilities, and time. To love him and to love people. Simple. Powerful.

God calls us to take joy in him and to move forward with boldness and courage. Yes, there are changes, but what *hasn't* changed?

Our identity in Christ. Our *security* in Christ.

Oh, friends, this is the bedrock of our hope. Our days on this present earth are but a shadow of our glorious future. On the timeline of eternity, this life is a tiny speck!

Let's nurture an attitude of anticipation and keep our focus on the goal. May Romans 12:10–11 be our heart's cry as we leap into our tomorrows with confidence. "Be devoted to one another in love. Honor one another above yourselves. Never be lacking in zeal, but keep your spiritual fervor, serving the Lord."

The God who makes a way in our wilderness and provides refreshing streams in our wastelands, remains faithful and true. He calls to us and extends a loving, steady hand. "Whether you turn to the right or to the left, your ears will hear a voice behind you, saying, 'This is the way; walk in it'" (Isaiah 30:21).

Reach for the God of renewal and get ready to soar. May the adventure continue!

Lord Jesus, with trembling excitement I stand ready. I long to truly live—to cherish my moments and to flourish in your loving faithfulness.

Use me, Lord! Teach me. Mold me into your likeness, into a girl after your own heart. In awe, I offer praise—praise for the call to deeper waters and a life of holiness. Thank you, precious Father. Oh, how I love you!

In the Zone

Write a letter of praise to the God of refreshing renewal. Ask for strength and courage to welcome each day with Christ-centered wonder and anticipation. Tuck your letter in a special place and remember to add praises on your journey.

About the Author

Leigh Ann Thomas is passionate about encouraging women to seek God's best. She has penned four books, including *Ribbons, Lace, and Moments of Grace—Inspiration for the Mother of the Bride*, an Illumination Award Medalist from SonRise Devotionals. She is a contributing author in twelve books and compilations, including *When Calls the Heart to Love* by Brian Bird and Michelle Cox from BroadStreet Publishing Group, LLC.

A staff writer for the parenting sites, InTheQuiver.com and Just18Summers.com, Leigh Ann has also written for *Southern Writers Magazine, Southern Writers Best Short Stories, Power for Living*, Charisma's *SpiritLed Woman*, and others.

She is married to her best friend, Roy, and they are thankful for the gifts of three daughters, two sons-in-law, three amazing grandsons and a grand-princess. They love their mountains-to-coast home of North Carolina where they are active in the ministries of Cool Springs Baptist Church in Sanford.

You'll find Leigh Ann on adventure with her sweetheart, getting silly with her grands, or daydreaming story plots on the front porch. Connect at www.LeighAThomas.com.

Notes

[1] https://www.ncpedia.org/jockeys-ridge-state-park

[2] https://activechristianity.org/comparison-is-the-thief-of-joy

[3] https://www.focusonthefamily.com/lifechallenges/managing-money/gods-big-ideas-about-finances/eternal-perspective

[4] https://www.mayoclinic.org/healthy-lifestyle/stress-management/in-depth/stress-relief/art-20044456

[5] https://www.christianquotes.info/quotes-by-topic/quotes-about-laughter/#axzz5W1CuTLRK

[6] https://www.audleytravel.com/us/blog/2010/may/unusual-plants-and-trees

[7] https://www.focusonthefamily.com/parenting/adult-children/bless-your-grown-children

[8] https://www.goodreads.com/quotes/94202-there-are-no-if-s-in-god-s-world-and-no-places

[9] Ten Boom, Corrie. 2006. *The Hiding Place,* Thirty-fifth Anniversary Edition. Grand Rapids, Michigan: Chosen Books.

Made in the USA
Coppell, TX
23 September 2021